The Secular Terrorist:

How Britain Conspires in its own Destruction

Peter Mullen

ISBN 978-1-901-54632-3

Cover Picture
Alina Reyes
Oil on Canvas
by Stephen Chambers
1998

St. Matthew Publishing Ltd
1 Barnfield, Common Lane, Hemingford Abbots
Huntingdon PE28 9AX   UK
01480 399098
Email: PF.SMP@dial.pipex.com
www.stmatthewpublishing.co.uk
Printed by Digital Book Print. www.digitalbookprint.com

The Secular Terrorist:

How Britain Conspires in its own Destruction

Contents

The Secular Terrorist:
How Britain Conspires in its own Destruction

Preface: We are our own worst enemy

What follows was prompted — you might even say provoked - by three recent influential books concerning the challenge which militant Islam presents to the West   Michael Gove's excellent essay *Celsius 7/7*; *Londonistan* by Melanie Phillips; and *Islam: The Challenge to the Church* by Patrick Sookhdeo. These are lucid and brave books in which the authors speak directly, treating their readers as adults; and none of the authors eviscerates his or her message according to the fashionable canons of Political-Correctness. In the last chapter of *Celsius 7/7*, Gove asks the question, "What is to be done?" And on almost his last page, he answers his own question:

"We also need to rediscover and re-proclaim faith in our common values. We need an ideological effort to move away from moral relativism and towards moral clarity, as well as a commitment to build a truly inclusive model of British citizenship in which divisive separatist identities are challenged and rejected".

Well, you might respond, so far so good. But Gove stops short of spelling out what our common values actually are. I met him recently and put it to him that we certainly don't need any more "ideological" efforts: during the last hundred years we have suffered from ideologies more than enough. So what precisely is required?

I am convinced the only "rediscovery" that can save western society is the rediscovery of our Judaeo-Christian civilisation and culture. Nothing else will

I

do. We cannot work up a programme of resistance to the enemies who assail us by vague aspirational talk about "models". And to call for "moral clarity" without spelling out what that clarity is *about* is to leave the job half-done.

What needs to be done is nothing less than a return to the practice of our faith. This is what the Jewish prophets in the Old Testament and the Gospels and Epistles in the New Testament consistently demand:

"Rend your heart and not your garments, and turn unto the Lord your God: for he is gracious and merciful, slow to anger and of great kindness" - *Joel 2:13*

"If we say we have no sin, we deceive ourselves and the truth is not in us. But if we confess our sins, he is faithful and just to forgive us all our sins and to cleanse us from all unrighteousness" — *I John 1: 8-9*.

Unfortunately we modern types suffer from a crippling delusion: we imagine we can have the peace and stability which comes through Torah and Gospel without having to go so far as actually to obey the commands and fulfil the obligations set out in those great texts. That modern prophet, T.S. Eliot warned us against this silliness back in 1934 when he told us that

"...such attainments as you can boast in the way of polite society will hardly survive the faith to which they owe their significance" — *Choruses from the Rock*

Gove asks for a "model". Eliot foresaw this craving for a wonderful scheme which, once implemented, would solve all our difficulties. And he scorned it as an act of futility, describing all such models and schemes as

"...men dreaming of systems so perfect that no one will need to be good" — *Choruses*.

"Dreaming of systems so perfect that no one will need to be good" — there is no better definition of the useless modern evasion we call Political-Correctness.

As a parish priest I have lost count of the number of times it has been put to me that we can have the civilisation which the Bible created without going to the trouble of believing what the Bible actually says. City types and Liverymen come up to me with a wry smile after the Sunday service and say, sometimes in as many words,

"The Bible may not be true − but it's a jolly good basis for society"

But, as I tirelessly point out, "Something that is not true is no basis for *anything*".

Among recent books which have responded to our crisis of civilisation, Gove's is one of the most apposite. There is another: *Without Roots* by Marcello Pera and Joseph Ratzinger. Ratzinger is the Pope and Pera is a professor of philosophy and former President of the Italian Senate. This is what Pera concludes:

"Christianity is so consubstantial with the West that any surrender on its part would have devastating consequences."

And he asks the crucial question:

"Will the Church, the clergy and the faithful be able to and want to be purified of the relativism that has almost erased their identity and weakened their message and witness?"

I would only expand Pera's category to include the Jewish Law and the prophetic tradition derived from ancient Israel. For Christianity itself was originally a sect which developed out of Judaism, and the New Testament is incomprehensible without the Old Testament. The relation between the Testaments is symbiotic.

As Gove has brilliantly pointed out, we face an uncompromising enemy and we must nerve ourselves to face it down. But I believe that the way we live in the

West today shows that we have lost our nerve. We have discarded the roots of our civilisation. In this sense we are our own worst enemy, for we constantly deny the only things that can save us. The early 20th century poet and philosopher T.E. Hulme (1883-1917) wrote:

"We have been beaten because our enemies' theories have conquered us. We have played with those to our own undoing. Not until we are hardened again by conviction are we likely to do any good. In accepting the theories of the other side, we are merely repeating a well-known historical phenomenon.

"The Revolution in France came about not so much because the forces which should have resisted were half-hearted in their resistance. They themselves had been conquered intellectually by the theories of the revolutionary side. The privileged class is beaten only when it has lost faith in itself, when it has been penetrated by the ideas that are working against it" — *Selected Writings*

"Our enemies' theory" is secularisation which involves, among other false doctrines, the belief that God is a primitive, outmoded idea, a delusion, and that modern man can devise his own ethical system, making up morals as he goes along on a merely utilitarian basis. I believe these suppositions to be destructive modern superstitions and that they constitute errors more deadly than anything they seek to correct. In fact secularism is fatal to western civilisation.

In March 2007, on the fiftieth anniversary of the signing of the Treaty of Rome which began the modern European movement, Pope Benedict criticised the EU as "godless." He spoke of Europe's denial of its Christian roots as "a form of apostasy" and he added:

"It is unthinkable that the EU could build a common European house while ignoring Europe's identity. Europe is a historical, cultural and moral identity before it is a geographic, economic or political reality. It is an identity built on a set of universal values which Christianity played a part in moulding."

Also, in the summer of 2007, the Archbishop of Canterbury, the Roman Catholic Archbishop of Westminster and the Chief Rabbi met urgently to discuss the threat posed to British society and culture by aggressive secularisation.

In the following pages I shall outline the progress of secularisation, how it has transformed Western society for the worse; how it has reduced us to impotence in the face of an alien fundamentalism which is confident and militant and which regards us as dross.

Systems and ideologies will not save the West. Have we the wit to recover our nerve and to return to the Judeao-Christian roots which alone can save us?

Peter Mullen, London 2009

I: Sex and shopping — The Social Revolution

How we were

Until comparatively recently, Britain was regarded as a Christian country. Its people thought of themselves, insofar as there was ever the need to consider such matters, as Christians. They were not devout. Churchgoing gradually declined from its peak in Victorian times and the rate of this decline increased after the First World War. The British people in the 20th century did not go in for family prayers before breakfast or for Bible reading after supper on Sunday. But, if you had asked them, they would have said they were Christian in the sense that they believed in "Do as you would be done by". Unconsciously they had imbibed the biblical morality exemplified by the Ten Commandments from the Old Testament and the Sermon on the Mount from the New. They were unostentatious, non-pious people whose overriding sense of decency derived from the Judaeo-Christian tradition which had shaped the lives and the institutions of Britain for more than a thousand years.

As a boy, I spent some time in hospital and I remember the cards affixed to the bottom of each patient's bed identifying that person's religion — presumably in case of the swift onset of a critical emergency. Some of these were marked "RC" and there were one or two here and there which said "Jewish". But the overwhelming proportion of them simply said "C. of E." I never recall any indicating that the occupant of the bed was atheist or agnostic. And this was in the 1950s, before the coming of the multicultural society and so of course there were none marked "Hindu" or "Muslim"

I grew up in the back streets of Leeds, between the renowned Armley jail and the New Wortley gasworks. Looking over the whole suburb was the tall black steeple of St Bartholomew's parish church. This was what was called "High Church" — vestments, candles, processions, smells and bells. My parents did not send me there for they regarded the High Church as "nearly Catholic" and therefore to be shunned as exhibiting "the mark of the beast". Not that my parents were scrupulous in the matter of religion. They did not go to church themselves but they sent my sister and me to Sunday School in the afternoons at the Methodist Chapel and back again in the evenings for Divine Service — partly because this was the "decent" thing to do with your kids, but chiefly so they could get a bit of peace and quiet.

Sundays were special. Most of the shops were shut — except my granddad's which was a newsagent. He could sell newspapers and cigarettes, but there were things he could not sell, such as the toys he sold all week and the small items of household requirements, saucepans, pan-scrubs and the like. Of course he *did* sell them, but with great surreptitiousness for fear of being detected by the "shop inspectors" and fined. Granddad's casuistry would have rivalled the Jesuits' or that of the old Rabbis finding intricate devices to get round the Sabbath laws. So for example, I once heard him say to a little girl who had come into the shop one Sunday to buy a doll: "I can't *sell* you that today, dear; but if you pay me £1 for this newspaper..." — it was the 1960s — "...I'll *give* you the doll for nothing!"

Children were not allowed to play out in the street but we were obliged to put on our smarter clothes, our "Sunday best". It was a day altogether more sedate. Most families, like ours, would end Sunday by taking an evening stroll into the park and listen to the brass band. Old men might be playing bowls there. But there was never any cricket or football.

Other days were different too. All the shops and factories closed on Good Friday. Even my granddad shut up shop, because there were no newspapers that day. Whitsunday was special. This Sunday, seven weeks after Easter, was in the north of England the day when children received their new clothes, their "Whitsuntide clothes". And the tradition was that children — boys as well as girls - went round the suburb to visit grandparents, uncles and aunts who would admire your new outfit and give you sixpence.

No one celebrated Halloween or Mothers' Day — still less the transatlantic novelty Fathers' Day. Christmas was kept joyfully but it started on Christmas Eve and not, as it seems these days at the end of September. And Christmas ended the day after Boxing Day when everyone went back to work.

The subdued and reticent 1950s were not much different from the 1930s or even from the 1910s. There were strict social conventions and public morality was conservative. Abortion was illegal and so was homosexuality. Divorce was still a social stigma. Of course, all these things went on, but abortions were "back street", everyone knew that there was a woman — in Armley she lived at 27 Hedley Street — to whom a girl might go if she "got into trouble". Occasionally there would be a homosexual scandal break in the newspapers, but these episodes were so mysterious that most people really didn't understand what was entailed. There were jokes about "bum boys" but, well, they were just jokes. In the rare event of a divorce, the couple involved were disapproved, as if somehow they had let the side down — like deserters from the battle.

In the space of a very few years, this settled way of life was changed forever.

Homosexual law reform

Homosexual practices were criminal offences until 1967 when Parliament, acting on the advice of the Wolfenden Report of ten years earlier, decriminalised homosexual acts committed by consenting adults in private. The key passage in the Wolfenden Report declared:

"Unless a deliberate attempt be made by society through the agency of the law to equate the sphere of crime with that of sin, there must remain a realm of private that is in brief, not the law's business" .

This was a humane reform and it was welcomed by the majority of the population who found distasteful the criminalisation of their fellow human beings for nothing more than the expression of their affections. Indeed until 1967 it was common for entrapments to take place, and homosexuals discovered *in flagrante* were often subject to blackmail and many careers and marriages were ruined. Homosexual law reform received support from all sectors of society including the churches.

But we should recognise what was actually decriminalised. The wording of the Bill specified homosexual acts "between consenting adults in private" where "between" meant two; "adult" meant that the two must be over twenty-one; and "private" meant behind closed doors. And of course the Act applied only to men. Homosexuality in women had never in recent history been a criminal offence

I doubt whether those who welcomed this reform would have voted for it if they could have seen where it has led forty years on. Gone now is all that restrained talk about privacy and adulthood. Now the love that once dared not speak its name screams at us in high camp on the high street on such brazen parades of homosexuality as so-called "Gay Pride Day." And nowadays, partly as a result of aggressive Gay lobbying and partly through further Acts of Parliament outlawing "discrimination", the public is meant to regard homosexual relationships as morally and socially equivalent to marriage.

No further changes in the law concerning homosexuality took place in England and Wales until the late 1970s.

In 1979, the Home Office Policy Advisory Committee's Working Party report *Age of Consent in Relation to Sexual Offences* recommended that the age of consent for homosexual offences should be eighteen. This was rejected at the time, in part due to fears that further decriminalisation would serve only to encourage younger men to experiment sexually with other men, a choice which some claimed would place such an individual outside of wider society. Subsequent amendments to homosexual offences legislation across the United Kingdom illustrates how this line of thought has developed rapidly, particularly in the new century.

First, the age of consent of twenty-one for homosexual males set by the 1967 Act was reduced to eighteen by the Criminal Justice and Public Order Act 1994. An earlier attempt by Edwina Currie MP to equalise the age of consent with that of the heterosexual age of consent of sixteen narrowly failed.

But then six years later The Parliament Act was invoked to ensure the passage of the Sexual Offences (Amendment) Act 2000 which equalised the age of consent at sixteen for both homosexual and heterosexual behaviour.

The Sexual Offences Act 2003, though subject to some controversy, introduced further changes in the way sexual offences are dealt with by the police and courts, replacing provisions that date back to the Sexual Offences Act 1956 as well as the 1967 Act. The offences of gross indecency and buggery have been deleted from statutory law and sexual activity involving more than two men is no longer a crime in the United Kingdom.

On 5th December 2005 it became legal for a same sex couple to register a civil partnership. Government guidelines for this ceremony reassure the couple:

"You will have the opportunity to say a set form of words before you sign the schedule. You will need to bring with you at least two other people who are prepared to witness the registration and sign the civil partnership schedule".

Thus a civil partnership is given exactly the same legal status as a marriage. They have become regarded in ordinary speech as "gay weddings" and advertisements abound for flowers, rings, receptions and the whole paraphernalia of the traditional wedding day. The Gay wedding is also regarded as morally equivalent to marriage and anyone who denies this is condemned as "homophobic" − a neologistic term which is not without its difficulties. For in the word "homosexual", "homo"- does not come from the Latin for "man" as is generally supposed, but from the Greek "ὅμοιος" which means "the same". So literally a homophobe is someone who is afraid of "the same" − a meaning and reference rather hard to pin down.

Moreover, what is indicated here is not merely a fear but an irrational fear or aversion: the proper comparison is with arachnophobia or agoraphobia. The implication is that anyone who is averse to homosexuality has a mental illness. The coinage of "homophobia" is therefore a political initiative of the sort identified by George Orwell in *1984* whereby language is changed to make those thoughts disapproved by the governing elite unthinkable, or at the least un-sayable. It is reminiscent of the Soviet and the Nazi propaganda machines.

The gay rights activist Peter Tatchell, who invaded the pulpit of the Archbishop of Canterbury as he preached one Easter Day, says, "Equality is not enough". On his website he claims,

"Lesbian and Gay freedom involves more than mere equal rights. Rejecting a simplistic law-reform agenda, queer politics celebrates sexual difference, opposes both assimilation and separatism, seeks social transformation and affirms that everyone is potentially queer".

Translated into ordinary English, this means that sexual orientation and behaviour should know no boundaries. Any human coupling — but why stop at the merely human? — is legitimate. Anything goes. Morality doesn't enter into it. Homosexual enthusiasts such as Peter Tatchell accuse those who uphold traditional Christian values as "moralising". Leaving aside for a moment the notion that moralising — making moral judgements — is one of the highest characteristics of human beings, what does Tatchell imagine his own position to be except that of a moral stance? For to say, as Tatchell says, that any form of sexual expression is legitimate is just as much a moral judgement as the Christian's statement, "All sex outside marriage is sinful".

Let us find a practical example to illustrate what is being asserted here. The public is being asked to allow that casual homosexual acts between (among) men who are such strangers to one another that they do not even know one another's names is morally equivalent to Christian marriage in which a couple, before God, makes a lifelong commitment "in sickness and in health, for better for worse, for richer for poorer, till death do us part".

Society used to value marriage above other forms of coupling, and governments of whatever hue preferred married couples in the system of tax relief. But, as even the BBC's website pointed out in December 2006:

"If you are thinking of getting married do it for love, not for any tax benefit - you would have to really scratch your head to try and find any big tax advantages to being married. The problem is that governments, of whichever party, decided many years ago that we should have all taxpayers treated separately for tax purposes. Hence the principle which existed in the past, that the husband and wife were a single taxable entity, has been systematically dismantled.

"There is now no married couple's allowance unless the elder spouse was born before 6 April 1935".

But casual Gay coupling — or casual heterosexual coupling if it comes to that — cannot be regarded as morally equivalent to marriage. For if morality means anything at all, apart from airy rhetoric and sentimentality, it means commitment and responsibility one to another. It follows that promiscuity debases those who practise it. But under the new secular dispensation and its politically-correct verbal lexicon, "promiscuity" is a word that is banned as "judgemental" and "homophobic".

Christianity recognises the fact that sex has moral consequences. First, as the Prayer Book says, "It was ordained for the procreation of children". Homosexuals are by their predilection relieved of this responsibility. The Prayer Book goes on to say that marriage is "a remedy against sin and to avoid fornication". Gay activists, with their moral doctrine of "Anything goes", do not believe that any act of sexual coupling can be sinful, and in the Newspeak that is political-correctness, they forbid the world "fornication" as "homophobic". Thirdly, the Prayer Book says that marriage was ordained for "the mutual society, help and comfort that the one ought to have of the other". It is difficult to see how this concept could be extended to include a five minutes' mutual masturbation session between/among strangers in a lavatory.

In the 1960s David Frost joked,

"They have made homosexuality legal. I'm leaving the country before they make it compulsory". It wasn't a very good joke even then, but it is barely a

13

joke at all today. In fact there has been a complete inversion of how we used to be before homosexual reform: whereas homosexuality used to attract censure, now it is "heterosexism" which is proscribed. Again this is doing violence to language and society in the style predicted by Orwell.

"Hetersosexual" is a word that came into use only with the process of homosexual reform. There was never a need for it before then. It was simply assumed, all unspoken, that heterosexuality was normal and homosexuality abnormal — where there was not necessarily any pejorative sense in the word "abnormal". Men go with women: that is normal. Men going with men: that is abnormal — i.e. in the prevailing mores of actual social practice. Now it is a thought-crime to assume that there is anything normal about sex between a man and a woman. That is the complete inversion.

There is a powerful argument for toleration of minorities, but what we have now is institutionalised intolerance perpetrated by the minority upon the majority. The social-religious reasons for the prohibition of homosexuality had their origin in the desire to protect marriage and the raising of children: that duty which every generation owes to its own and to the next — the provision of a stable society where, as it says in the marriage Service "Children may be Christianly and virtuously brought up".

Of course a homosexual couple *might* make vows of fidelity and bring up their adopted children immaculately. But there is nothing to say that they will. It is, after all, the view of total sexual permissiveness expounded by homosexuals themselves - such as Peter Tatchell — which renders all vows and promises, all notions of fidelity and permanence in sexual relationships, as having been displaced by the great homosexual liberation movement. Sex need have nothing to do with commitment. Sex is a leisure activity. What was once a mortal sin is now only a lifestyle choice. Self-gratification is the only moral law. You may not object to this. It is objecting to it that has been criminalised now.

And it must be assumed that the adopted or otherwise techno-biologically procured children of homosexual partnerships will be brought up according to the diktats of such as Peter Tatchell which insist that "Everybody is potentially queer" and that the social engineering project for which he is working so devotedly has actually been completed.

Homosexual law reform was originally welcomed by the great majority of liberal-minded people in Britain because it was recognised as designed to protect a persecuted minority. It has resulted in the abolition of sexual morality altogether. Buggery and sodomy are no longer criminal offences. Is there any sexual behaviour now prohibited? Paedophilia? For how long?

Abortion law reform and embryo research

In 1861 Parliament passed the Offences Against The Person Act. Section 58 of the Act made abortion a criminal offence, punishable by imprisonment from three years to life even when performed for medical reasons. No further legal changes occurred in England until 1929. Two successive laws, the Infant Life Preservation Act 1929 and Abortion Act 1967 provide the exceptions to this 1861 Act.

In 1929 the Infant Life Preservation Act amended the law stating it would no longer be regarded as a felony if abortion was carried out in good faith for the sole purpose of preserving the life of the mother. The Act made it illegal to kill a child "capable of being born live", and enshrined twenty-eight weeks as the age at which a foetus must be presumed to be viable. Importantly, the Act allowed a doctor to perform an abortion legally if he was "satisfied that the continuance of the pregnancy was liable to endanger the health of the expectant mother".

In 1936 the Abortion Law Reform Association was formed by people who believed that abortion legislation was unsatisfactory. The Association recommended that the law be clarified, as the 1861 Act still on the statute books deemed abortion illegal under all circumstances, while the 1929 Act allowed for abortion in exceptional cases.

In 1938 the Bourne case was an occasion for a change of policy on abortion. A young woman was gang-raped by a group of soldiers and became pregnant. Dr Alec Bourne agreed to perform an abortion for her and was subsequently prosecuted. Dr Bourne argued that it was necessary to perform the abortion to preserve the health of the young woman. The judge agreed that forcing her to continue with the pregnancy would have been tantamount to wrecking her life.

The doctor was not convicted. This case set a legal precedent for performing an abortion to preserve a woman's mental health.

In the time between the Bourne ruling and the 1967 Abortion Act, some women did have abortions for urgent medical reasons or, with the consent of a psychiatrist, to protect their mental health. Wealthier women were more likely to be able to pay to see a psychiatrist who could agree to a safe abortion, but many would still have had no option but to seek illegal methods for ending a pregnancy — resorting to "the back street abortionist".

The cost to women's health of illegal abortion was high with about forty women dying each year and many more seriously injured. Doctors, politicians and members of some religious communities argued for a law that allowed for abortion in certain circumstances. The Abortion Act was passed in 1967, a time of lively political campaigning, and is sometimes seen as one of the triumphs of the women's movement. The reality is that it was not passed to give women rights, but to respond to a public health problem.

The law gave the rights and responsibility for decision-making to doctors not pregnant women. It did not legalise abortion, but allowed for exceptions to the illegality of abortion. Much of the law is open to interpretation and asks doctors to make a judgement based on weighing up risks rather than specifying particular circumstances in which abortion would be legal.

There have been several attempts in Parliament to restrict abortion law further by those who do not support a woman's right to choose abortion. Those who do support the so-called "right to choose" are also unsatisfied with the law as it stands, which they regard as both vague and too restrictive. In 1990 the 1967 Act was amended by the Human Fertilisation and Embryology Act, which reduced the original time limit of twenty-eight weeks to twenty-four weeks for most abortions.

Today, though a large majority of people in Britain support the provision of legal abortion, there is still debate about the future of abortion law with several groups campaigning to reduce or remove the availability of abortion.

Recent debate about the Abortion Act has centred on two possible changes to current legislation:

(1) The removal of the need for a woman to seek permission from two doctors to have an abortion — in order to prevent unnecessary delays for women seeking abortion under 12 weeks.

(2) Further reduction in the upper time limit on abortion.

Reliable abortion statistics for the years before the 1967 Act are not available, but in the first year after the passing of that Act there were 22,332 legal abortions in England and Wales. By 1978, this figure had risen to 111,851. In 1988 there were 168,298. In 1998, 177,871 and in 2004, there were 185,415. Throughout this period the number of live births has declined drastically so that today the number of aborted foetuses represents one third the number of live births.

We remember that the prevailing argument in favour of abortion invoked the physical and mental health of the mother. Are we supposed to deduce that a great catastrophe has fallen upon women in the UK over the last forty years, so that nowadays seven times as many of them are in precarious states of mental and physical health as were in that condition in 1968? Of course not. The reality is that abortion is being used as a form of contraception.

As in the case of homosexual law reform, this development is an example of unintended consequences. Just as few who voted for the decriminalisation of homosexuality in 1967 ever envisaged the public parades of Gay Pride and the assertion that casual homosexual relationships are morally equivalent to marriage, so those who were persuaded that a woman should not be obliged to bear a child if by doing so her health would be seriously undermined, did not foresee a time when abortion would be regarded in effect as a mere convenience.

Sex education is taught throughout the schools and the contraceptive pill is freely available, and yet more women than ever seek abortions. The conclusion must be that they regard it as too much trouble to have to remember to take the contraceptive pill. In the "liberated" society why should there be even a moment's impediment to the gratification of desire?

Of course PC language is introduced to sanctify abortion, and it is done in an ingenious way. Our democratic, emancipated, modern and progressive way of life vastly approves the idea of choice. So let the subject of abortion be discussed under the slogan "The woman's right to choose" — which is, being interpreted, just another way of saying "Choice" = "Abortion." Interestingly, abortionists develop this theme further and speak of a woman as "having the right to do as she wishes with her own body". Perhaps she has this right. But the fact is that the embryo is *not* her own body.

This is curious. Throughout society children are sentimentalised. A visiting alien would conclude from our rhetoric and through the cosy movies that are constantly being made concerning children, that we are a nation which adores its offspring. But this is only rhetoric, only sentimentality. When it comes to it, the unborn child is disposable if its birth is regarded as an inconvenience in the life of its mother. There is an even more curious corollary: the same pressure groups that campaign for abortion on demand are notedly strongly opposed to capital punishment for acts of murder. That is to say, they believe in killing the innocent and freeing the guilty.

If any embryo whose existence is deemed to be *inconvenient* may be aborted, what moral stricture stands in the way of killing a two week old child for the same reason?

As in the case of homosexual law reform, so with abortion, there has been a revolution in traditional mores, a revaluation of values leading to practices which make today's world unrecognisable from that of forty years ago. And again the driving force behind this revolution is secularisation, the deliberate disregarding of our historic Christian tradition and practice.

The Marriage Service says that marriage "is ordained for the procreation of children". The Bible celebrates children:

"Lo, children and the fruit of the womb are an heritage and gift that cometh of the Lord. Like as the arrows in the hand of the giant, even so are the young children. Happy is the man that hath his quiver full of them" (*Psalm 127:4-6*)

That is to say, the Judaeo-Christian civilisation regarded children as holy, as beings in their own right, as ends in themselves and not as disposable impediments to the progress of hedonism.

Most of what has been said in the case of abortion applies also to embryo research which is defended on the grounds that such experimentation will lead to some future goods, specifically to the prevention and cure of disease and deformity. But this kind of moral reasoning is utilitarian and the good that it seeks is hypothetical, not yet realised; whereas the embryos involved in the research are living and actual. Classically, Christian theologians have always argued that it is not permissible to do evil in order that good might come of it.

Specifically in the Catholic Bishops' document *Cherishing Life* they say:

"*In vitro* fertilisation raises issues about procreation and parenthood, but it also raises concerns about society's attitudes to the lives of those embryonic human beings it creates. ~ While in principle every embryo conceived in the laboratory could be transferred to its mother, in practice of the many conceived only a proportion are given the chance of life. ~ Most are discarded or frozen, perhaps to be transferred later, perhaps only to be discarded or used in experiments. ~ This is a great injustice. ~ Even worse is the practice of conceiving human embryos for the sole purpose of scientific experimentation".

And *The Catechism of the Catholic Church* says

"Since it must be treated from conception as a person, the embryo must be defended in its integrity, cared for, and healed, as far as possible, like any other human being."

On the fashionable subject of "cloning" again in *Cherishing Life* the Church is quite explicit:

"It has recently been suggested that cloned human embryos could be used as a source of stem cells which could be useful in future medical advances. This is usually termed 'therapeutic cloning' though it would not be therapeutic for the cloned embryos who would be destroyed for their cells. The process is also euphemistically called 'cell nuclear transfer' a title which disguises the fact that the aim is to produce human embryos and then make use of them. Therapeutic cloning would be far worse than full pregnancy cloning as it would set up a system in which human embryos were cloned only to be destroyed so that their cells could be 'harvested'. Medical research which involves the destruction of human embryos is a crime against their dignity as human beings. It should also be noted that there are good alternative sources of stem cells which do not require cloning or the destruction of embryos. Stem cells taken directly from adults are already being used in medicine and appear to represent the most promising way forward for stem cell therapy".

Insofar as the supporters of embryo research consider that any justification is required for their utilitarian ethics, they argue in favour of their utilitarian ethics that the embryo is "not a person", and they conclude from this that therefore the embryo is disposable, that it may be used as a means to a greater good. But the point is that while of course the embryo is not a person – neither in the fullest sense is a three months old child – no embryo left to develop has ever become anything *other than* a person. It is certainly a human being. What else could it be? "Embryo" is shorthand for "a human being in embryo." The question is whether it could ever be permissible to kill a human being, a potential person, in the interests of some future and hypothetical good?

What does it say about a society which is prepared to do this? Certainly it says that such a society is one that has no room for the Christian doctrine of creation and humanity. In other words, it is a secular society without any sense of transcendent or ultimate value: a society in which the very concepts of right and wrong are not absolute but variable according to the benefits they might produce. But beneficial for *whom?* Certainly not for the unborn. Beyond this, even what may be adjudged a "benefit" depends on moral criteria of some sort.

Why do secularists imagine that their criteria should be assumed as the only ones and so go all unchallenged?

Christian versus secular is a subject that lends itself to dispute and argument, but, beyond argument, there is something intensely visceral — the Christian would say *incarnated* — about it. For we are not talking about abstractions here. We are talking about an actual society, a community of human beings, a fellowship in which we live, move and have our being. And so it becomes more than a theoretical argument. It is a matter of existential choice: which society do you choose — the Christian or the secular? Are you at ease in a society which treats its unborn as utilities? As F.R. Leavis said on the issue of morality and choice: "Show me what you value, and I'll tell you what you're worth."

Divorce law reform

Divorce was not legalised until 1857 and before that date an Act of Parliament was required to obtain a divorce. The 1857 Matrimonial Causes Act permitted divorce for the innocent party where their spouse had committed adultery. The grounds for divorce were extended in 1937 to include desertion, cruelty and incurable insanity. The 1969 Divorce Reform Act widened the grounds still further to include unreasonable behaviour and kept the three previously existing fault grounds. The 1969 Act in effect provided for divorce without fault on the grounds of "irretrievable breakdown" of the marriage. Few respondents contested petitions for divorce and the numbers of dissolved marriages increased greatly

The Family Law Bill of 1995 declared that divorce should be seen as "a process over time" and the minimum period allowed was one year. So "no fault" divorce was passed on a free vote in both Houses of Parliament.

In 2003 there were 166,700 divorces in the UK, more than half of them involving children under sixteen. In 2001 11.5% of children lived in households headed by a divorced or separated parent. In 2007 the number of children living in one-parent families has tripled since 1972 and the number of such families has risen from four million to twelve million. A fifth of children who saw their parents divorce in 2005 were under five, and two thirds were under ten.

There have been consequences. The average cost of divorce is now more than £25,000 and forces one third of divorcing couples to sell the marital home when they split up. A report filed in 2000 estimated identifiable welfare costs of family breakdown at £8.5 billion and the total direct costs to the taxpayer of at least £15 billion. In a Green Paper *Supporting Families*, the government acknowledged that "rising crime and drug abuse are indirect symptoms of problems in the family. Of the 60,000 children currently in care, 98% are there owing to family breakdown.

In his book *English Ethical Socialism*, A.N. Halsey, Professor of Social Policy at Nuffield College, Oxford, writes:

"No one can deny that divorce, separation and birth outside marriage and one parent families as well as cohabitation and extramarital sexual intercourse have increased rapidly. Many applaud these freedoms. But what should be universally acknowledged is that the children of parents who do not follow the traditional norm (i.e. taking on personal, active and long-term responsibility for the social upbringing of the children they generate) are thereby disadvantaged in many major aspects of their chances of living a successful life. On the evidence available such children tend to die earlier, to have more illness, to do less well at school, to exist at a lower level of nutrition, comfort and conviviality, to suffer more unemployment, to be more prone to deviance and crime and finally to repeat the cycle of unstable parenting from which they themselves have suffered. The evidence all points in the same direction, is formidable and tallies with common sense"

Even the progressive Joseph Rowntree Foundation reported in 1998 that broken families have a higher risk of:

(1) Being in poverty and poor housing

(2) Being poorer when they are adults

(3) Behaviour problems

(4) Performing less well at school

(5) Needing medical treatment

(6) Leaving school/home when young

(7) Becoming sexually active, pregnant or a parent at an early age

(8) Depressive symptoms

(9) High levels of smoking, drinking and drug use

Every research finding I have come across in my reading for this chapter concludes that where there is an increase in the numbers of broken marriages there is a corresponding increase in social breakdown. These findings take into account only the empirical evidence. Theological and religious arguments have not even received a mention. So it seems indubitable that, even on the utilitarian grounds preferred by secular social reformers, the increase in the divorce rate has been and continues to be a disaster for society.

You might think that, noticing the social benefits of marriage, any government would do all in its power to strengthen the institution. But, in 2007, the Chancellor of the Exchequer repeated his refusal to offer tax-relief to married couples. Mr Brown said:

"I mean practical, sustained help, whenever and wherever families need it, in whatever circumstances they find themselves; not by making ideological judgements but seeking always to find the best way to support every child".

It is a perverse mentality which refers to the institution of marriage, a cornerstone of civilised life in this country for two millennia, as something based on an *ideology*. But perhaps Mr Brown should be excused: for those who are conditioned by their political experience to believe that life itself must be lived out according to the ramifications of an ideological struggle cannot help but think in ideological terms. But it is a way of thinking which dehumanises the "honourable estate" of matrimony.

It is now illegal to teach the Christian doctrine of marriage in schools. Legislation passed under new equality laws in 2006 and 2007 decree that it is no longer permissible to teach that marriage is the normal, natural and institutional relationship, prescribing the union of one man and one woman for life. It is permitted only for teachers to say that *some religions* believe that marriage is the only proper institution for sexual relationships. It is probably, or soon will be under the same regulations, illegal for the parson to preach against adultery and sodomy. This measure, backed by all the main political parties, gives to homosexuality and casual heterosexual relationships the same status as marriage.

When we open the Bible and the Prayer Book, we see there that "Matrimony is an honourable estate instituted of God in the time of man's innocency, signifying unto us the mystical union that is betwixt Christ and His Church... and is commended of St Paul to be honourable among all men: and therefore is not by any to be enterprised nor taken in hand, unadvisedly, lightly or wantonly to satisfy men's carnal lusts and appetites like brute beasts with no understanding; but reverently, discreetly, advisedly and soberly and in the fear of God; duly considering the causes for which matrimony was ordained."

And the first of those causes is children, the procreation and the care of children. By locating marriage in the counsels of God, our Christian predecessors stressed its importance. By dislocating sex from marriage and human coupling from the begetting and raising of children, progressive secularism has made immediate gratification and personal pleasure its first consideration. Children are, as it were, accidental by-products or side-effects of a value-free leisure activity. The personal and social dereliction lies all around.

The Abolition of Religious Education

Before the late 19th century, all schools in the UK were church schools and, with the exception of a very small number of Roman Catholic establishments, this meant they were Church of England. Children were brought up to learn the Catechism in *The Book of Common Prayer* and they were prepared for Confirmation.

RE maintained its strong place in the curriculum after the various Education Acts of the period including the important Forster Act of 1870 which made elementary education statutory for all children. But the Forster Act provided that RE should be nondenominational: i.e. Christian education was compulsory, but it was not to be according to the tradition of any particular church or sect. Christian basics taught in this period typically included the stories of the Patriarchs from the Old Testament, the Gospels and the missionary journeys of St Paul, the Lord's Prayer and the Ten Commandments. Collects from *The Book of Common Prayer* would be learnt "by heart" — a humane expression now supplanted by the mechanical "by rote". This practice was underwritten by the Butler Education Act of 1944

Succeeding Acts drafted since the advent of the so called "multicultural society" have lessened the Christian emphasis. For example the Education Act of 1996 says:

"Religious Education must reflect the fact that the religious traditions in Britain are in the main Christian, while taking account of the teachings and practices of the other principle religions".

There are crucial distinctions here. For instance, until the 1944 Act was modified by later Acts, "religious education" was taken to be a subject containing actual knowledge and truth — like mathematics or geography. And that knowledge and truth was Christian. In other words, it went without saying that Christianity was taught as something that was *true*. Acts subsequent to 1944 have relativised the teaching of religion, so that now the Christian faith is not taught as something that is true: instead pupils are taught *about* Christianity. In the words of the 1996 Act Christianity is "taken account of" alongside other world religions.

I have been involved in RE in state schools as a teacher paid not by the church but by the Local Education Authority. I have been a member of the legally-constituted Boards set up by various LEAs and I have observed how RE is actually taught in schools today — where it is taught at all, for it has to be admitted that many schools flout the law and do not teach the subject.

Many parents will be disturbed to know that OFSTED, the school inspectorate, recently reported that four out of five secondary schools do not obey the law and hold a daily act of worship for their pupils. This gives young people the message that it is perfectly acceptable to disobey any law that may be regarded as inconvenient. As yet, no serious action has been taken against any law-breaking school by any of the responsible authorities.

RE has become less Christian, even less religious, and more anthropological, and it tends to take the form of a global survey of what people believe: "Buddhists believe this, Hindus believe that and Muslims believe the other — what do you believe, Sharon?" And typically Sharon is thirteen and has very likely had no experience of religion of any sort.

The logic of this method of doing RE is hardly ever followed to its conclusion: that such a method is bound to be secular. For the only way you can teach *about* religion(s) is from a perspective that lies beyond religion(s) — the secular and even atheistic perspective. This is underscored by the fact that most teachers do not themselves practise any religion. It is actually illegal under the terms of the 1996 Act to teach Christianity *as true*. So in the space of sixty years RE has been completely revolutionised and secularised.

If any teacher should attempt to teach Christianity as true, he might well find himself accused by the secular establishment of "indoctrination". But again logic is not followed to its conclusion: for only to teach *about* religion means to indoctrinate with secular prejudices. The widespread "progressive" or "liberal" assumption is that to teach Christianity is to seek to inculcate outdated and groundless dogmas and prejudices; but to teach from the secular perspective is a mark of neutrality and impartiality. In reality the unspoken premise is that the secular perspective and secular values are the only true ones. In effect, religion is regarded as primitive superstition, something which people "used to believe".

Moreover the content of RE in many schools displays a particular and consistent bias: Crusades - bad; missionary activities abroad — nasty imperialist expansion; the Great Wars — unnecessary and the only heroes the pacifists; hero worship of liberationist/socialist icons — Ghandi, Martin Luther King, Nelson Mandela; the uncritical acceptance of the slogans of environmentalism and the unassailable truth of the dogma of global warming; bewailing the slave trade, instead of rejoicing that it was Christian campaigners who abolished it — while of course neglecting to mention that the biggest slavers of all were (and are) the Muslims.

No more Sunday, Christmas or Easter – or Christian Europe

It became legal in 1994 for small shops to open all hours on Sundays and for large shops – supermarkets and the like – to open for any period of six hours between 10am and 6pm. This Act of Parliament was one of the clearest examples in modern times of shutting the stable door after the horses had bolted for, as the BBC reported at the time:

"The new law is not expected to herald a large increase in the number of stores open on a Sunday as many had broken the old law for years".

Town centres used to be peaceful places on Sundays and you could enjoy a walk through them and notice the buildings uncluttered with business, the streets quiet and the shops shut. Now the towns are if anything busier on Sundays than weekdays. The pubs are open all day long as well.

One of the greatest social benefits of traditional Christian observance was to give the nation one day in the week to get its breath back, a day of rest and quiet recreation, a gratifying contrast to the noise and rush of the working week. That has gone and we are beset by a hectic commercial monotony seven days a week. Professional spectator sports are played too, so that someone wrote in a Sunday newspaper a few years ago: "The football fan has two Saturdays in the week now!"

It must at least be questionable whether making all the days in the week exactly alike is an unmitigated benefit to the people. At any rate the abolition of Sunday, the weekly festival and reminder of the resurrection of Christ, has removed conscious recollection of the saving work of Jesus Christ from public consciousness. This constitutes one of the brashest and farthest-reaching examples of gross secularisation.

Good Friday, Easter and Christmas retained much of their character as Christian festivals until comparatively recently. I recalled earlier how when I was a boy there were no newspapers on Good Friday and even my granddad's newsagent's shop was shut. Not now. And the fact is rarely remarked on. But is it not a huge change in national life and culture when we see that the chief event in the Christian faith – the redemption of the world through the

Crucifixion and death of Our Lord and Saviour Jesus — is utterly disregarded in public life? You might think that even a nation which had slackened the rules about Sunday observance would cling to the essentials — in other words that *something* would remain sacred. But nothing remains sacred. That is what "secularisation" means. And surely there must follow profound psychological changes — amounting even to deprivation — in a population from whom all recollection of what is sacred has been removed?

Easter and Christmas have been commercialised. But those festivals were always commercial opportunities. More importantly, they have been de-christianised. The analogy is with homosexual law reform and the change in public consciousness which followed it. At first homosexuality was tolerated, but then any suspicion that it was being *merely* tolerated was derogated as "heterosexism". Rather in the same way, any insistence in the public realm that Christmas is fundamentally Christian is condemned as "offensive to people of other religions".

In fact no one has ever come across a devout Muslim who is "offended" by the Christian celebration of Christmas — or a Jew "marginalized" by the churchgoing which takes place at Easter. Rather, the claim that Christian festivals offend people of other faiths is an excuse, a lie perpetrated by aggressive secularists to disparage and reduce Christian influence in British society yet further.

The observation of Sunday as something like a Christian Sabbath, together with the other principal Holy Days of the year, was a living symbol of an underlying social reality: testimony to the fact that Britain was a Christian country, not through strict doctrinal tests on its people but as a nation founded on Christian values. The continuing understanding until comparatively recently was that these standards form as it were the conscience of the nation. "It's not Christian" was on a par with "It's not cricket."

All this has now disappeared, with predictable deleterious social consequences. The old easy-going Christian settlement did not despise a man for having a drink or taking a bet; but twenty-four hours drinking, bingeing by the middle class and government appointed casinos would never have been tolerated even by that most tolerant and un-emphatic version of Christianity which has been the moral bedrock of our country since the Middle Ages.

As I write, there is an exhibition of *Hogarth's London* in one of the galleries. One need not pay for admission. Scenes worse than anything depicted by Hogarth make up the daily life of the capital — and of towns and cities countrywide. There is widespread drunkenness. But I have observed it at first hand here where I work as a City Rector at the heart of the financial centre. It is not cheerful drunkenness. It is desperate, nihilistic. Pretty young women, exquisitely turned out, earning top salaries in banking, insurance, the law and public relations go out in gangs on many nights in the week with the single determination to get uncontrollably drunk — as they say, "Like totally out of it." Their expectations are desperate too. It is not just a case of a riotous night on the tiles: every time they set out it has to be "The best ever". And as I walk through the City streets on my way home from church at night, there are these pretty young women vomiting into the gutter and crying because their lives are in chaos, meaningless.

Forty years ago City men wore pinstripes and bowlers and read *The Times*. Now they go hatless and dress down. They still read *The Times*, but this is what *The Times* advertises on a typical day:

"Tonight sees the return of a series that delights in the description 'The Black sheep of Channel Four's flock'. It is aimed fairly and squarely at a young post-pub audience and it's basically no more than a dangerous variation on *Candid Camera*.
"Among its attractions is 'the annoying devil' dressed in red PVC who pours water on top of a woman who has just had her hair done. A couple of idiots hurt each other with darts and snooker balls. A man hurls junk food at unsuspecting members of the public. A house-hunting couple make out in front of the estate agent and a female interviewer humiliates celebrities. The audience whoop and cheer throughout".

I read this and turned for relief to St Augustine, *Civitas Dei, Book II:*
"The people are unconcerned about the utter corruption of their country. 'So long as it lasts,' they say, 'so long as it enjoys material prosperity why should

we worry? What concerns us is that we should get richer all the time and have enough for extravagant spending every day. Full publicity is given where shame would be appropriate; close secrecy is imposed where praise would be in order. Decency is veiled from sight; indecency is exposed to view. Scenes of evil attract packed audiences; good words scarcely find any listeners. It is as if purity should provoke a blush and corruption give ground for pride."

St Augustine in his time looked on all this and prophesied there would come a reckoning. It did come, in the form of the downfall of the Roman Empire and the descent into the Dark Ages. Looking out over the Western world today — a world which, like Rome, has barbarians at the gate and moral squalor within — can anyone doubt that there will be for us too a reckoning?

Drink, drugs, gambling, sexual promiscuity in which any coupling (tripling, quadrupling?) is acceptable and a debauched mass media which has the population in thrall to a shabby, mindless and voyeuristic celebrity culture: that is the social milieu of post-Christian Britain on the edge of a new Dark Age. I was on the Eurostar to Paris the other week, among a group of well-dressed, well-off City bankers. They opened their briefcases and took out their reading matter for the journey: *Hello!* Magazine and something worse called *Heat*. By their fruits ye shall know them. Look at what they value and you can soon tell what they're worth.

In every area of national life and social policy the Christian faith is less prominent today than it was fifty years ago. The traditions which have shaped our nation for more than a thousand years are being dismantled and undermined. This is happening not because of some great public outcry, some national distaste for our Christian way of life, for the obliteration of our Christian character. It is the deliberate policy of a hostile establishment, a secularising elite intent on a programme of "modernisation" by which it is intended to remove all traces of the Christian inheritance from the public realm and influence.

The next chapter will consider the church's response to secularisation.

II: What has the Church done?

The swinging sixties and theological iconoclasm

Fifty years ago the condition of the Church of England was a cause for thanksgiving. The Church was in good health and in good spirits. In the 1950s post-war boom there was actually a religious revival: congregations were increasing, the numbers being baptised and confirmed were up and particularly vocations to the priesthood were flourishing in all sections of the church — high, low and broad. I was one of three men in our parish of St Bartholomew's, Leeds who offered themselves for the priesthood towards the end of that decade. And St Bartholomew's parish was a working class district, not some refined rural idyll from where sons of, if not the gentry, then at least the better off might be expected to "go into the church".

Thanks to some imaginative publishers, there was a boom also in Christian literature of a very high quality and all in affordable paperbacks. C.S. Lewis' hugely readable apologetics series including *Mere Christianity, Miracles* and the delightful *Screwtape Letters* were best-sellers. J.B. Phillips was another popular Christian writer, producing lively modern translations of the Gospels and The Acts of the Apostles. Spiritual classics were being published also in paperback at two shillings and sixpence (twelve-and-a half pence!) a copy: such as Kierkegaard's *Journals*; G.K. Chesterton's *Orthodoxy*; Gerald Vann's *The Divine Pity* and *The Confessions* of St Augustine. It was an encouraging time to be a young Christian: to be an ordinand was very heaven.

This happy trend continued for the first part of the 1960s, but then the unrelieved decline began. I was myself training for the priesthood by that time and I remember vividly the onset of the revolution which has proved the destruction of the traditional Church of England.

The main cause of this destruction was theological innovation, a sustained process of debunking the ancient doctrines of the faith. The word used at the time was "demythologising" – a concept invented by Professor Rudolf Bultmann of Marburg and swiftly popularised by British theologians such as Bishop J.A.T. Robinson and Dr Alec Vidler. Robinson's *Honest to God* was a paperback sensation. Robinson said that a God who is "metaphysically out there" is as incredible as a God who was erroneously thought to be "up there".

To many this looked like a declaration of practical atheism. The fact that it was a bishop saying these things gave the impression of the cat being let out of the bag. Most British people at that time would have called themselves Christians in the sense that they believed in "Do as you would be done by", but many had their doubts about the existence of God. Now here was a bishop confirming their doubts in another famous Robinson slogan, "Our image of God must go". We were being told that our traditional belief was really childishness and we must grow up. This was emphasised in another phrase much quoted in *Honest to God* – Dietrich Bonhoeffer's description of modern man as "come of age".

It was an early symptom of a habit of thought which became prevalent – wholesale contempt for the past. As if the biblical writers and the Church Fathers were quite good in their way, but not half as clever as we modern types; as if St Paul and St Thomas Aquinas were mere primitives compared with the come of age theologians of the 1960s.

This theological iconoclasm seemed at the time to be a natural part – the church's part – in the general climate of irreverence which characterised the 1960s. For the first time since the Edwardian music hall, Britain could boast its own culture of popular music and design: *The Beatles*, along with such as *Gerry and the Pacemakers* creating "the Liverpool sound" which became massively more popular than borrowings from the USA – where our pop music traditionally came from. There was the invention of "swinging London" and the worldwide triumph of British design epitomised by Mary Quant, the King's Road boutiques and the miniskirt.

At the same time there was the eruption of a phenomenon which became known as "satire" — though it was not anything that Aristophanes or Jonathan Swift would have recognised under that name. Really it was bawdy disrespect and its most sensational success was the late night Saturday television show *That Was The Week That Was* which mocked and ridiculed all prominent politicians and particularly the Tory government of Harold Macmillan who, with his tweeds, moustache, passion for shooting grouse and his relaxed patrician drawl, was an obvious target for the new irreverence.

British politicians traditionally had been the recipients of deference. Live interviews on radio and television were rare, but when they did occur they followed the pattern of a deferential reporter saying such as. "Good morning, Minister. I wonder if you could spare a minute to tell us something about the government's policy on…" - as it might be the shipyards, the atomic bomb or the plastics factories. The new, mocking tone came as a shock to the politicians, but the public, worn out by the war, the post-war austerity, regulations and shortages were delighted by what seemed like if not quite liberation, then a massive outbreak of lightening-up.

TW3 as it became known was also sexually risqué with Millicent Martin playing the vamp while singing rude songs about our political leaders and indeed about all those who had become accustomed to having us regard them as our elders and betters. Then at the height of all this hilarity came the Profumo affair in which a Cabinet Minister had been caught consorting with call girls. All the salacious ingredients combined: glamour, sexy parties, drink, the hint of the kinky and the exotic, drugs and Russian spies. All these things combined to produce a giddy, cheerful atmosphere in which the public believed that at long last the pretence was over, the game was up, the politicians and aristocracy were as lustful, craven and indisciplined as the next man. The people noticed this — and they rejoiced. I know. I was one of them.

All the taboos were being blown away. Even Harold Macmillan himself, speaking about foreign policy, had heralded "a wind of change" and told the public at home they had "never had it so good" — a phrase which echoed in many smutty jokes concerning the participants in the Profumo affair. There was book censorship at the time, but this too was soon to go the way of everything that was old, stuffy and repressive. The newspapers and television enjoyed themselves in their coverage of the so called Lady Chatterley trial in which the uncensored publication of D.H. Lawrence's sordid, class-conscious bodice-ripper was debated in the High Court. Much amusement was generated when the judge demonstrated just how out of touch he was with the new mood by asking a witness, "But is this the sort of book you would like your wife — or one of your servants — to read?"

So called "four letter words" appeared in *Lady Chatterley's Lover* and this was a great novelty, because no one — certainly no member of the suddenly more prosperous working class — had ever seen them written down before, except on the lavatory wall. Teenagers went about gleefully quoting the lugubrious, sex-obsessed Lawrence: "I like a lass as pisses and shits" and "By, tha 'as a lovely cunt". It was all good entertainment of the upstairs and downstairs sort as, in Lawrence's silly book, the gamekeeper was having it off with the mistress of the house. O what fun! O what insubordination! At that time also the louche theatre critic Kenneth Tynan uttered the word "fuck" for the first time on television. And this on Reith's BBC! There was, as it were, the feeling that the whole country was caught with its trousers down — and moreover no one minded in the least

John Robinson naturally became "the swinging bishop" and the sense was of the church also joining in the fun of casting off the former stuffiness and "getting with it". It was the era of curates in jeans riding *Lambretta* motor scooters, playing table tennis with the youth club and sweating through late night discussions with them at the diocesan retreat houses on the rights and wrongs of "heavy petting". Teenagers were not at that time deemed ready (even by themselves) for full sexual intercourse: most of them were virgins until marriage, or at least until they became engaged to be married. But *Honest to God* and the other debunking popular theological books were only the mild beginnings of a process of iconoclasm which became more ruthless and extreme as the decade wore on. In a series of books such as Harvey Cox's *The*

Secular City and Paul Van Buren's *The Secular Meaning of the Gospel*, we were urged to adopt "Religionless Christianity". It was all part of the general radical chic of that flashy and trivial decade. There was even a title *The Gospel of Christian Atheism* by Thomas J.J.Altizer.

Specifically, the debunking theologians denied the Virgin Birth and the Resurrection along with all the miracle stories of the Bible. They took their cue again from Bultmann's quaint pronouncement, "You can't believe in the miracles and the Resurrection in the age of electric light and the wireless". And no one dared ask — like the child pointing out the emperor had no clothes — "Why not?" Really, the new theology was only slogans and propaganda. The fashionable debunkers distinguished between "The Jesus of History and the Christ of faith" — in which Jesus was represented as an unlikely amalgam of Che Guevara and Mahatma Ghandi and the Christ of faith was a childish myth.

When the new theologians were asked to account for the long history of the Christian faith and how it had survived if its basic revelation and teaching was phoney, their answers were in the form of psychological explanation. For example, the first disciples did not actually witness an empty tomb and Jesus risen from the dead. It was just the case that somehow, after his death, they suddenly realised the significance of his person and teaching and were "filled with new life". When you pressed the new theologians, "But if Jesus was dead and remained dead, where did the sense of new life come from?" — they could not give a satisfactory reply.

So you might become even bolder and ask how, if the disciples knew that Jesus had not in fact risen from the dead, could they bring themselves to preach that he had? Was the whole gospel a lie? Moreover, was it a lie so powerful that even the disciples were deceived by it — deceived to the extent that they were prepared to be persecuted and even go to their deaths for proclaiming it? This seemed preposterous.

The whole of the New Testament was "demythologised" in this way. The new theologians spoke of this method as if it was an act of cleansing — removing all the miraculous which "modern man come of age" found so troublesome. Take the Virgin Birth of Jesus for another example. The modernisers did not believe this of course. Their argument against was curious and you might almost say *ignoratio elenchi*, irrelevant, beside the point. They noted that many ancient societies and cultures had believed in virgin births and these belief were myths or legends. They concluded from this that the New Testament account of the Virgin Birth of Jesus must be part of a myth or a legend also. But there is no logical backing for such a deduction. As Chesterton said, "Sceptics did not disbelieve in miracles because their freedom of thought allowed them to disbelieve. They disbelieved because their very strict materialism did not permit them to believe".

There are arguments against miraculous happenings — most of them easily refuted - but the new theologians did not apply any of them. They simply disbelieved out of pure prejudice — the prejudice revealed in Robinson's contemptuous title *But That I Can't Believe!* Why not? The new theologians never ceased reminding us that the Gospel writers were "men of their time" with all the thought-forms and intellectual fashions of their time. But the new theologians did not stop to consider that *they* too were men of *their* time, with their own collection of prejudices. This prejudice was against the supernatural. It was simply assumed that the category of supernatural beings and events was something outdated, something that had passed away. We had outgrown it. This prejudice was entirely suited to the 1960s with its mania for everything new.

The 1960s were also a period of political radicalism. There were the race riots in America and the student rebellions in France and on a lesser scale in Britain too. Feminism brought promises of women's liberation. The fashionable heroes were Fidel Castro and Che Guevara, the assassinated John F. Kennedy and Martin Luther King. The whole sense was that the old order of things was being done away with and we were reckoned again to be on the verge of some bright new age. As Wordsworth had written of the French Revolution:

"Bliss was it in that dawn to be alive: and to be young was very heaven"

That would make a wry epitaph for the swinging sixties. God too was secularised and became a metaphor for revolutionary politics — or at least for the ecclesiastical version of *radical chic*. Jesus was a first century Che and the church even printed posters depicting him as such.

All you need is love: the new morality

Along with theological nihilism came what was called at the time, specifically as the title of chapter six of *Honest to God*, "The new morality" — which one traditionalist critic dismissed as "Only the old immorality in a miniskirt". Under the new morality, the Ten Commandments were discarded as obsolete authoritarianism which may have been suitable for Moses and primitive desert tribes but which were quite inappropriate for "man come of age".

What was proposed instead was "situation ethics", an extreme form of act utilitarianism in which we were recommended to make moral decisions on the spot, in the "situation" according to "the demands of love". But without the Commandments, without ethical precedents of any sort, without even rules of thumb, "the demands of love" were left unhelpfully vague. The new morality was the church's version of *The Beatles'* song, *All You Need is Love*. It went with those embarrassing newspaper photographs of archdeacons doing the twist and curates on motorbikes, of Bishop Robinson himself turning up in court to support the overturning of the ban on *Lady Chatterley's Lover*. That dear old maiden aunt D.H.Lawrence: English literature for not quite grown-up people.

In the catchphrase of the period, the church was "getting with it". *Heilige Geist* was replaced by *Zeitgeist*. Churchmen persuaded by the new morality were naturally vigorous in their support for the sexual revolution which decriminalised homosexuality, made divorce much easier and legalised abortion.

How did it come about that the church was able to discard its traditional moral code as if throwing out a chest-full of worn vestments? The Judaeo-

37

Christian moral heritage was inscribed at the beginning of every service of Holy Communion in the words of the Ten Commandments which the priest read out to the congregation and the congregation responded by asking for God's grace to keep them. I suggest two answers. First, anything so authoritarian as a Commandment went right against the grain of libertarianism that was the signature of the 1960s. God must on no account be regarded as having authority: that would make him just a supernatural version of the "imperialist" leaders of the western world. And, after all, Christians were supposed to be freedom-fighters now — like Fidel and Che and Ho Chi Minh.

Radical chic and teenage rebellion are passing phases perhaps — though it is astonishing how they manage to seduce each succeeding generation into thinking they are novel. But there was a far deeper prejudice and a more pervasive influence behind the new morality: the doctrine of progress. For a century the main currents in western thought had taught evolution, development and forward movement. Following Hegel, Marxism was an historical creed in which the future is all mapped out according to the principles of dialectical materialism: the revolution, the workers' control of the means of production, the Marxist utopia (as a sort of secularised heaven) and the punishment of the capitalists. It is a pity that the scholars and churchmen who took so readily to the pastime of debunking historic Christianity did not apply themselves rather more thoroughly to exposing the intellectual vacuity and utter worthlessness of the determinist view of history.

Alongside Marx sat Darwin, and it was not long before the belief in the physical evolution of the species was attended by the belief in our moral evolution. Herbert Spencer, George Bernard Shaw and T.H. Huxley were three of its notable prophets. People in the 1960s believed above all in progress. Off with the old and on with the new. We were all come of age and had no need for the ancient prohibitions which were in any case far too "negative". *The Beatles* even had a song about it: *Getting Better All The Time*.

Progress was the great delusion of 1960s consciousness, and it must be said that it has hardly abated since that time. What is truly astonishing is that a belief in human progress and moral perfectibility could exist alongside an acquaintance with even the outline of 20th century history. The terrible battles of the First World War, the Somme, Paschendaelle, the Menin Road – twenty million dead. The Second World War, the fire bombing of Dresden and Hamburg, unimaginable carnage and cruelty on the Russian front, the concentration camps and the mass murder of six million Jews – with Hiroshima and Nagasaki for a fitting climax to the proceedings. The Korean War. The war in Vietnam. The genocides perpetrated not just by Hitler but by Stalin who murdered forty million of his own people and Mao who killed seventy million.

The 20th century – the century that believed in progress and getting better all the time – saw more people killed in wars and revolutions than in all the wars and revolutions of history put together. It is eccentric of modern progressive people in the mass media, that whenever they want to refer to an event as especially evil, they describe it as "medieval". They really ought to use the word "modern" if they want to be accurate.

There were 20th century theologians and churchmen who had recognised the persistence of human wickedness and the delusory nature of progress – Karl Barth in Switzerland and D.R. Davies in Britain - to name just two. But such men were out of fashion. For example, Karl Barth's great study of sin and redemption, his portrait of St Paul entitled *Romans* was published in 1914 – the same year that the First World War broke out. In a college essay I thought I was being smart when I quoted Alec Vidler's comments on Barth's *Romans*: "It fell like a bomb on the playground of the theologians". I recall my tutor wrote in the margin of this essay: "There weren't enough decent theologians even to fill a playground".

The belief in progress was irrationally bolstered by technological innovation. We are back with Bultmann's remarks about what we can't believe in the age of electric light and the wireless. In less than a century we had come from a man on a horse to a man on the moon. We had radar, radio and television, antibiotics, tourism flights worldwide, effective deodorants, indoor plumbing and frozen fish fingers. What in the face of these modern wonders were dirty, old-fashioned things such as wickedness and sin?

The western world was in denial and the church blessed its delusions.

Liturgical reform: you couldn't make it up

Following the demythologising of Scripture and the discarding of the Ten Commandments, the church's third act in the destruction of the traditional church was liturgical reform. *The King James Bible* and *The Book of Common Prayer* were sidelined and replaced by numerous modern translations of Scripture and by the new forms of service published in instalments as booklets and called *Series One, Two* and *Three*. The new Bibles and the new services were banal and unmemorable except for the unintended humour in them. Who, for example, but a modern churchman could think that a passable substitute for "Arise, take up thy bed and walk" is "Take up your pallet and go home". The drama and rhythm of the first is supplanted by something that only sounds like advice to a sloppy painter.

"Compassed about" became "surrounded", which makes us think not so much of angels and saints but of wagon trains and Red Indians. For "wolves in sheep's clothing", we were offered the pantomime howler "men dressed up as sheep". *The King James Version's* sublime "pearl of great price" is rendered in the vocabulary of a *Blue Peter* presenter as "a pearl of very special value". The abyss into which the mind of the modern church has descended is exemplified in a few words from the newest form of the Marriage Service in which the priest prays (croons?) over the couple. "Let them be tender with each other's dreams"

We ought at least to start by attempting to be fair to the liturgical revisers and grant them integrity in their efforts. What did they think they were doing? A statement from the Liturgical Commission of the Church of England in 1979 sets out its aims: "We wish to provide forms of worship that are intelligible to the people of the 1970s. The language of the 1662 *Book of Common Prayer* is outstandingly beautiful, but no one speaks like that now. We are producing services in the language of today".

40

This statement is not true either in what it claims directly or in what it implies. No one ever spoke in the street the language of *The Book of Common Prayer* (1662) and the *Authorised Version* of the Bible (1611) - any more than ordinary folk in medieval times went around saying "Quoth", "Prithee, good knight" and "Gadzooks!" We can safely leave that sort of utterance to Hollywood historical epics. Rather, from the beginning, the language of those books was set in a particular register, recognisable as the religious register.

This way of addressing God in prayer was meant to be preserved over time and that is what happened. The Prayer Book and the old Bible were hallowed by time and use and their vocabulary infused ordinary speech and raised even the way we speak four hundred years later to the level of poetic utterance. A few examples: "fell on stony ground"; " erred and strayed"; "miserable offenders"; "till death do us part"; "ashes to ashes"; "daily bread"; "lighten our darkness"; " our bounden duty"; " the devil and all his works"; "born again"; "fell by the wayside"; "mutual society, help and comfort"; "with this ring I thee wed"; "in sickness and in health"; "all my worldly goods"; "dust to dust"; "the twinkling of an eye"; "vile body"; "devices and desires" etc.

I could have filled pages with these examples, for I did not have to scratch around to find them: they are the permanent residue of English religious consciousness. They are like our landscape. Noting that the Old Bible and the Prayer Book were written in the 16th century when the English language was at its richest, freshest and most vivid, W.H. Auden remarked, "How lucky we are! Why spit on our luck?" That question was for the benefit of the liturgical reformers who were doing away with the old books — books which the Anglican Divine Jeremy Taylor praised as "the treasure-house of rare devotion".

And so they are a treasure-house, a matchless, one almost wants to say *miraculous*, repository of spiritual consciousness, phraseology which lies at the very centre of human psychology and defines what it is to be a human being. These books answer to our deepest needs and they have done so for four hundred years. They are words for all seasons, a place to go when the need to

41

express joy or sorrow, birth, marriage, death, guilt, heartache, loss and fear becomes unavoidable. To borrow the words of the lager advertisement: *The King James Bible* and *The Book of Common Prayer* refresh parts which modern versions cannot reach.

One disastrous consequence of the discarding of the old books is that no one, especially the children, knows any prayers or sacred texts by heart any longer. The revisers have achieved a form of practical atheism. They have obliterated the religious register, the very distinctive tone of English Christianity. Phrases that once lurked in the unconsciousness of even the most un-churched among us have been taken from us. The result is a terrible spiritual deprivation, so terrible that it might be described in the words of Scripture itself: "An enemy hath done this thing"

The liturgical revisers were not even competent. They were not poets or literary men. They were bureaucrats, "modernisers" made in the same mould as the enthusiasts in New Labour who set themselves for a decade to modernise British society to the point of destruction. But whereas New Labour did not quite succeed, the Church bureaucrats have achieved total victory: they have expunged the forms and shapes, the echoes and rhythms of English Christianity from the minds and hearts of the people. What sort of people were they, these liturgical revisers? Thomas Cranmer's words for the works of their predecessors in the 16th century remain remarkably apposite for today's liturgical and theological philistines:

"…Vain attempts and impetuous assaults by such men as are given to change, and have always discovered a greater regard to their own private fancies and interests than to that duty they owe to the public".

The Alternative Service Book (1980)

The ASB was the culmination of twenty years labour in the back rooms and corridors of the General Synod. It was a hugely costly production with a marketing budget of half a million pounds — a colossal sum thirty years ago.

And it is worth pointing out that this money came out of the contributions of the people in the parishes to central funds. It was a church tax for the purposes of funding innovation. How good was it? Could it be considered a worthy successor to the *BCP*?

I will turn first to the family offices — Baptisms, Marriages and Funerals — for these are the services which have the most influence not on the wholly committed who attend every week but on the great majority of occasional churchgoers. In *The Book of Common Prayer* weddings were conducted according to a rite titled *The Solemnisation of Matrimony* The *ASB* changed this to *Marriage Services* - like "customer services" — as if they didn't believe that marriage is solemn any longer. The *BCP* introduction to this rite includes vivid phrases of extraordinary beauty and tenderness such as:

"...which holy estate Christ adorned and beautified with his presence and first miracle that he wrought in Cana of Galilee".

But in the *ASB*, gone is the holiness, gone is the adorning and beautifying and, of course in the newly demythologised church, gone is the miracle and we are baldly informed that Christ himself,

"...was a guest at a wedding".

Not even the guest of honour, mind you. Was there ever a clearer case of wine into water?

The *BCP* included all those serious and stern words about marriage "as a remedy against sin and to avoid fornication". But in the inoffensive, sugary rite in the *ASB* these essential elements in the Christian teaching about marriage have been done away. The couple are no longer invited to enter into holy matrimony

"reverently, discreetly, advisedly, soberly and in the fear of God"

For "the fear of God" is replaced by "serious thought". As my ten year old son remarked at the time, "But dad, you could have serious thought about cricket!" Leaving out all mention of God is atheism by stealth if not quite (or not yet) atheism by decree.

In the *BCP* the priest warns the couple:

"I require and charge you both as ye will answer at the dreadful day of judgement when the secrets of all hearts shall be disclosed…"

This is among other things a caution to the couple against bigamy and other forms of unlawful marriage. That the new book omitted all reference to the day of judgement should come as no surprise: revisers who can abolish "sin" and "the fear of God" will have no trouble getting rid of the prophecies of Christ about the end of the world and the certainty of God's judgement. But the form of the revised caution to the couple has been so euphemised and bureaucratised that it no longer has any moral or spiritual force at all:

The priest says instead: "I am required to ask". It is like a final note from the Inland Revenue.

When it comes to the giving and receiving of a ring and the joining of hands, the *ASB* reveals its utter lack of understanding of what is going on. The *BCP* says simply, "With this ring, I thee wed" — six words of one syllable, going back to the time of Chaucer when they were said at the church door. These are words which I, as a priest who has solemnised hundreds of weddings, know exactly fit the movement, the drama, as he puts the ring on his bride's finger. Incredibly, the *ASB* makes him say instead:

"I give you this ring as a sign of our marriage"

Eleven words for six. Was this done, I wonder, because we were reckoned not to be able to *understand* the original? The extra words are tedious and redundant. The poetry is lost. The drama is destroyed. The rhythm is obliterated. Besides, if the groom has to *tell* his bride that the ring is a sign, it means the sign isn't working: imagine the motorway and, "This is a road sign saying etc etc..." You would have crashed the car by the time you had read it.

The Burial of the Dead has become *Funeral Services* and it appears as if the chief aim is to avoid as much mention of death as possible. Even cheerful, hopeful lines are left out. Take that proud, confident statement which the priest used to pronounce as he led the coffin down the aisle:

"I know that my Redeemer liveth and that he shall stand at the latter day upon the earth".

It is thrilling. The response of every funeral congregation I have ever attended is to stand up immediately. Those are words of faith made more faithful by their connection to Handel's wonderful aria from *Messiah*. So why leave them out? The reason soon becomes obvious: those words are followed in the original by,

"Though after my skin worms destroy this body"

And a book which dare not mention "fornication" and "carnal lusts" will hardly bring itself to the remembrance of "worms". But the forfeiting of the line about "worms" means that the profound faith of the next line must be given up as well. So the *ASB* cannot say,

"Yet in my flesh shall I see God".

This is a loss of nerve followed by something much worse: the emasculation of the Gospel and the loss of faith.

I remarked earlier that one of the greatest benefits of memorable liturgy, repeated day in and day out over the centuries, is that words and phrases from it enter and enrich ordinary language. Here is an example from *The Burial of the Dead*: the novel title *Vile Bodies* by Evelyn Waugh. The *BCP* says of Christ that he, "…shall change our vile body"

But the genteel, euphemistic, unreal *ASB* dare not mention vile bodies. What — corpses at funerals? Whatever next! But because the *ASB* will not mention vile bodies, it must lose the next and wonderfully assuring line,

"…that it may be like unto his glorious body".

But because there is no death in the *ASB* funeral, there can be no room for the Resurrection either. It is the mourners who are being punished here by the revisers who first remove all death's terrors and then remove Christ's promise of everlasting life.

What is the Baptism for? The *BCP* is clear: "the mystical washing away of sin". But the *ASB* does not believe in anything so *negative* as sin, still less in "the devil and all his works". In the *ASB* Baptism, the devil is not so much mentioned, let alone renounced. We feel we want to ask the compilers of this shoddy theological text, "If there is no sin and no devil, from what, for God's sake, did Christ come to redeem us?" Actually, things are rather more complicated. The revisionary theologians and liturgists do not do away with the concept of sin entirely. Instead they contrive something which makes no logical sense: they remove the notion of *personal* sin but retain the idea of *corporate* wickedness. So "We are all to blame" for our country's imperial past, for the slave trade, for world poverty and climate change — just don't mention the hurtful remark you made to someone at work or the lie you told your wife. Incidentally, the Baptism in the *ASB* is called "Initiation Services" which, I'm afraid will only make people think of witchcraft films on late-night television.

Remember Evensong? Glorious Evensong, country churches and, in Eliot's lovely words,

"So, while the light fails
On a winter's afternoon, in a secluded chapel
History is now and England".

The most evocatively mesmerising spiritual line in Evensong is:

"Lord, now lettest thou thy servant depart in peace, according to thy word"

The *ASB* deletes this and offers instead: "Lord, now you let your servant go" — which sounds not so much like a man in distress of soul, as a schoolboy in distress of bladder. There are so many other infelicities and desecrations that they seem almost casual, wanton destruction of what is beautiful — like a nasty little child pulling the wings off a butterfly. Who in his right mind could alter "thou that sittest" (in the Gloria in Excelsis) to "you are seated". Is that any way to speak to God? "Seated" — it is like "Please be seated. The manager will see you shortly". "Seated" where? Up and a little bit to the left of the Liturgical Commission's filing cabinet?

It is the register that is all-important. This is a matter of literary, poetic — even musical — skill. But the compilers of the *ASB* all have tin ears and they don't know what religious English is. They don't know, for instance, the elementary difference between an affirmation and a denial. For example, at a high point of The Holy Communion we have in the *BCP* the English translation of the ecstatic Latin text:

"Sanctus, Sanctus, Sanctus Dominus Deus Sabbaoth"

"Holy, Holy, Holy Lord God of Hosts"

Followed by: "It is very meet, right and our bounden duty..."

But unbelievably the *ASB* renders this line as, "It is not only right..."

So at the high point of the High Mass, the *ASB* gives us anticlimax, bathos, by replacing an ecstatic affirmation with a dreary denial, a "very" with a "not".

We recall that the church authorities trumpeted the arrival of the *ASB* as "The greatest publishing event in four hundred years". Twenty years later the same authorities officially *banned* it. In 2000 the *ASB* became, ecclesiastically speaking, a forbidden book. First, this bears out what its critics had said all along: that it was rubbish and that as such it couldn't last — not even two decades. Secondly and far more importantly, it says something about the character of the modernisers: they are the people who call themselves "liberal"; those who ban books are not liberals but totalitarians. Book-banning? We think of Berlin in 1933 and the bonfires of literature and modern science which Hitler's thugs made in the streets. It is ironic that the same generation of church reformers who so enthusiastically called for the lifting of the ban on the third rate novel *Lady Chatterley's Lover* should actually impose a ban on a prayer book.

Given the debacle of the *ASB*, what might intelligent modern churchmen have learnt from it? Surely that they were not competent to compose new church services and that therefore they should turn to those who were competent. The first place one would look would be to the compilers of *The Book of Common Prayer* — formative religious texts which had penetrated the minds and hearts of English people for centuries. But that was not the method of the liturgical reformers. They began again the task of producing yet another modern prayer book.

The dog returns to its vomit.

Common Worship (2000)

C.H. Sisson described the ASB as "the book of variants" because its orders of service are not concise or integrated — as are say Morning Prayer and Evening Prayer in the *BCP*. They are rather series of endless alternatives in which the worshipper is forever being invited to turn to page "N" for the alternative canticle, reading or eucharistic prayer. There was a perpetual rustling of paper at an *ASB* service as worshippers follow instructions to find the appropriate prayer from the myriad alternatives. But compared with its successor, *Common Worship* the *ASB* was a masterpiece of concision. The promotional literature for *CW* describes it as "Twenty-three sections under six headings". In fact it is not a book at all, as we understand the meaning of the word, but a collection of texts which you can buy at the religious bookshop or download from the *Common Worship* website.

As Kingsley Amis prophesied, "More will mean worse".

No one could accuse the *ASB* of taste and elegance in expression, but *CW* excels even that volume in verbal clumsiness and in accommodating itself to the trashy therapeutic newspeak of modernity. The worshipper might easily imagine he is being talked (down) to by the presenter of a children's television programme. Parents and godparents, turning up to have a child baptised, for instance are informed:

"This is a demanding task for which you will need the help and grace of God".

Didn't they know this already — that baptism is a Sacrament and therefore a serious business? Do they have to be told, as it were, to make sure they are paying attention? Then they are regaled with a full dose of that therapeutic, touchy-feely newspeak — language which of course belongs not to the religious register at all but to the secular world of counselling:

"God invites you on a lifelong journey...Christian formation must allow an individual's story to be heard".

This is narcissism, a prescription for psychotherapeutic onanism.

Those who produced this new Baptism service offer with it a commentary in which they say in a section headed *Accessible Language*:

"The full and rich imagery surrounding Baptism and the comparative ignorance of this imagery in many sections of modern society pose a major problem in the drafting of services of Christian initiation".

"The comparative ignorance of modern society". I feel like asking, "And whose fault is that then?" Perhaps it is the church's fault. But never mind.

Given this ignorance of "full and rich imagery", the revisers' solution is to abandon the imagery and its richness; whereas a better solution would be to present the full and rich imagery so that modern society might become acquainted and eventually enriched by it. People have to be taught. But by their relentless dumbing down, the revisers refuse Christ's commandment to go into all nations teaching and making disciples.

There is a curious rite in *CW* called *Emergency Baptism*. I know what an emergency Baptism is: it is what I have on occasions been called out to perform — to baptise a baby who is thought to be unlikely to survive. *CW* would not have us feeling queasy about this. It says:

"Parents should be assured that questions of ultimate salvation or of the provision of a Christian funeral do not depend on whether a child has been baptised"

In other words, when is an emergency not an emergency? Answer: when it is an emergency Baptism. There is a new prayer which demonstrates just how far the liturgical revisers are from understanding what makes for acceptable English, what forms of words are appropriate in a prayer and which phrases belong elsewhere entirely. This new prayer begins:

"I see water flowing from the threshold of the temple"

I fear this will only provoke wits in the congregation to call out, "Quick — call the Ecclesiastical Insurance Company!"

The Marriage Service is frankly laughable. But isn't making holy things an occasion for amusement a kind of blasphemy? The bridegroom at the chancel step has to say to his bride:

"All that I am I give to you"

What — does he give her his bad temper and his indigestion? Those words don't belong in church. They belong in a sentimental pop song and lend themselves to crooning. Worse, the priest prays,

"Let them be tender with each other's dreams"

That belongs in a very *bad* pop song. We recall the lugubrious Diana-fest and *Candle in the Wind*. I think that in *CW*, beside those schmaltzy words, there ought to be a rubric in the margin:

"The congregation shall now throw up: bride's family's side first".

The *CW* Funeral Service makes me afraid to die. I should hate to have the words found in it spoken over even my corpse. The service contains a reading in which the Gospel says, "Jesus wept". But *CW* has only "Jesus was moved to tears" — as if he had been watching for the umpteenth time Leonardo di Caprio and Kate Winslett on *The Titanic*.

Again we are given the *Blue Peter* lecture:

"There is a real sense of loss at the death of a loved one" At this low point, satire becomes impossible.

Again it says, "Lord be with us as we open the door". The mourners will laugh, surely? If only it had said, "Lord be with us as we open the box" — we could at least have imagined ourselves as contestants in a macabre TV quiz show.

Occasionally the revisers fail to distinguish between words appropriate to a technical theological discussion and words suitable at a religious service for ordinary members of the public. One of the prayers begins:

"We have this treasure in earthen vessels to show that the transcendent power belongs to God"

The technical word "transcendent" has no place in something which after all is called *Common Worship*. Besides, is such a technical word thought to be "accessible language" to people who are assumed to have difficulty with "With this ring I thee wed"?

The *BCP Burial of the Dead* contains the awesome expression, "Though worms destroy my body". *CW* renders this, "After my skin has been destroyed" — what, through sitting too long in the sun outside the funeral parlour?

Another prayer begins with the clumsy and inappropriate invocation, "Intimate God". You might, at a pinch, say "Dear God". But what does "Intimate God" suggest? God as sex-counsellor? The prayer then descends to the sub-Freudian,

"Reconcile us through your Cross to all we have rejected in ourselves"

That is an ugly phrase but, worse, it is poor theology. For there are things we *ought* to reject in ourselves: our sins for instance. The prayer after a suicide says, "Hear our prayer for those in despair". What if they are not in despair but trusting in God?

Probably the worst part of this very bad book is the Order for Holy Communion — or I should say of course the *Orders* for Holy Communions: for like the devils, they are legion. Whereas it seemed too much of a feast when the *ASB* gave us four eucharistic prayers, *CW* has eight on offer. In the *BCP* we find the Prayer of Consecration begins movingly, "In the same night that he was betrayed, he took bread..."

CW says, "He had supper with his friends". What Chinese, Indian or just a pizza? The heartbreaking spiritual and human intensity of Christ's sufferings is here rendered banal.

The left-wing, social gospelling bias which we noticed earlier in considering the new theology that emerged in the 1960s is well-represented in *CW* where, to take just one example from many, it says that Jesus "was born in poverty in a manger". Our Lord was not born in poverty: his earthly father Joseph was a tradesman and of the middle class. Besides the circumstances of Jesus' birth are irrelevant to the truth of his Incarnation — that greatest of all condescensions. The revisers seem to think that for God to have been born in relative poverty is somehow a greater condescension than if he had been born Mayor of Stockport — or even if he had chosen to be born as Czar of all the Russias. The same political leanings are evident in the Harvest Prayers where we are urged to pray for "the sins of our society".

In the revisers' Introduction to Common Worship entitled *Planning for Change: Suggestions and Ideas*, it says:

"When the *ASB* was published, no one knew which (if any) of the new services would stand the test of time"

Twenty years: it is an eccentric notion of what constitutes the test of time. The *BCP* has stood that test for four hundred and fifty years.

An infantile clergy — the bishops worse

The travesty of worship which I have just outlined is not the worst of it — not by far. Most parish churches do not even use the inferior styles of liturgy to be found in the *ASB* and *Common Worship.* Parishes are actually encouraged by central authority to "do their own thing." And, if a parish does decide to abandon the *Book of Common Prayer* and refuses to break the law by persisting with the *ASB*, the only formal respite available is to concoct its own services from *CW.* This is not straightforward — because *CW* was not published as a single volume between two covers, but in dribs and drabs as the fertility of the minds of the liturgical revisers allowed. So we were invited to go along to the church bookshop and buy booklets and pamphlets of the new services as they came out. Or, of course, the Church of England being in the vanguard of technological modernity, we could download the new rites from the Liturgical Commission's website.

So parish worship was turned into a new Babel. The *BCP* was a compromise document hammered out of the religious wars and controversies of the 16th and 17th centuries and, until the late 20th century, it was used by all the main parties in the Church — High, Low and Broad. The Tractarian John Henry Newman prayed by means of it, so did his theological opponent the Evangelical Charles Kingsley, and so did the Broad churchman Dean Inge. The Restoration ideal worked in practice and it turned out as the compilers of the *BCP* had hoped and intended: "…that all the nation shall have one use."

Today, you cannot go into two parish churches in adjacent villages and expect to find that they use the same (or even a similar) order of worship. Instead you will find the local customised usage, a scissors-and-paste job in the form of a booklet, bits and pieces downloaded from *CW*, stitched on next to "that prayer from the *ASB* that we all like so much," together with any bits and pieces that take the Vicar's fancy.

And even when the service starts, it will be constantly punctuated and interrupted by injunctions to, "Turn to the form of Confession on page three" or "…use the fifth Eucharistic prayer on page nine." Also the priest will provide something like a running commentary of verbal admonitions such as, "We shall now proclaim our faith by saying together The Nicene Creed." Whereas the priest used simply to begin, "I believe in one God…." and everybody else joined in. This redundant chatter ruins everyone's devotions. The words used in prayer should be prayers and nothing else.

The result of all the downloaded alternatives and local customised uses mean that there is effectually no longer such an institution as The Church of England. The parish churches throughout the land have all gone their different ways and they have nothing in common. Thus *Common Worship* is a misnomer. There is no worship held in common. The C. of E. is in reality now merely a congregational church. This is destructive of our mission and evangelism because it has removed all consistency from public worship and obliterated even the possibility that any prayers might lodge in the mind and take root there.

To what could you compare this pandemonium? Imagine if every football team in the country played the game according to its own customised rules. There could never exist such a thing as a football league. And all the mindless commentary interjections interpolated by the priest of the "We shall now proclaim our faith etc" just disjoint the fluency of the service and remove the sense of a religious pace and rhythm. The secular injunctions — stage directions — by the priest get all mixed up with the words of the liturgical rite. It is a kind of sacrilege. No poetry remains. There is no longer the beauty of holiness. The glory has departed.

But even these atrocities are not the limit of liturgical degradation. The bishops, synodsfolk and modern clergy — that gang of advisers and apparatchiks who are in charge of the non-parochial (though paid for by the parishes) quangos which run the C. of E. these days — relentlessly encourage us all to "experiment with worship." Let us, then, enter the heart of darkness…

Recently, all the clergy in the diocese of London were called to a "Sacred Synod" at the Low Church shrine of All Souls, Langham Place — next door to Broadcasting House. The church was packed. It was billed to start at ten-thirty, but when I got there at about twenty-past it was already in full swing. The conductor was on the rostrum conducting the orchestra in the sort of sub-Lloyd-Webber sounds that seem to have taken over church music these days. The clergy were belting out what the programme called *the gathering songs.* Homogenous musical pap. Sentimentality set to a tired rhythm. And the clichéd modern hymns written by tin-eared rhymers.

> *The glory of Jesus majestic to see*
> *Up high on a mountain transfigured was he.*

Di-diddle-di-diddle-di-diddle-di-dum. Reminds you of those songs of our misspent youth concerning ladies from various parts of the country. Other songs were just embarrassing:

> *All within me falls at your throne.*

It suddenly struck me that I'd come across this conductor before: he features a lot in a publication called *Hymns for Today's Church*. In this book there is a hymn which begins, *Lord be with me in my depression* which surely ought to be re-titled, *Who would true valium see.* There was the conductor leaping about on the podium trying to get the three hundred parsons to sing up. This sort of thing is meant to be cheerful, but it doesn't work. The glee was so lugubrious: his expression was like lust recollected in impotence. Imagine the face that Mr Sowerberry, the undertaker in *Oliver Twist*, might pull upon learning that he had just won the National Lottery. Given the wall-to-wall carpeting and the soapy music, the effect was of a pop concert in a crematorium.

The theme was Epiphany. So why not include the beautiful Collect for Epiphany from *The Book of Common Prayer*, then? But no, all the prayers were of the contrived modern sort of prose that drags along like a lump of dead meat. *As we gather in prayer from across the Diocese of London...* Giving geography lessons to the Creator of the world. Then *Almighty God, we thank you that we have been inspired by the Holy Spirit...* You could have fooled me. If the Holy Ghost is really supposed to be behind all this stuff, why is it so fifth rate?

But these trials were only a prelude to the real horror: *The Presentation of the London Challenge Video.* Towards the end of one of the prayers, a white screen slowly descended and obscured the portrait of Our Lord which forms the reredos. Think of the lowering of the safety curtain at half time in the Christmas pantomime at the Sunderland Empire circa 1958 and you'll have it about right. Instantly, there was a loud blast of heavy rock music and the video began. It was supposed to be a tour of what the churches are doing throughout the diocese. In the whole presentation there wasn't one extract from a traditional service — not a single, recognisable gobbet of religious sanity.

We visited a service performed by a group called IGNITE. (Well, you could wish). The leader was a young evangelical rocker who said, *We teach biblical truth but we're flexible about the cultural thing.* Which, being interpreted, means, *We want to strip from our form of worship anything that might be contaminated by the Christian tradition of the last 400 years.* So they produced more pop music and everybody jigged about. Has he never heard of Marshal MacLuhan, this evangelical rocker who wouldn't be seen dead at a traditional funeral: *The medium is the message.* If the Christian faith is presented in incomplete sentences and ugly music, it will cease to be the Christian faith. Because the Christian faith is that supremely beautiful thing.

The video took us next to a church which was grotesquely overlit where the priest was turned out in vestments which would have looked well on the Captain of the *Starship Enterprise.* And there was more dancing. After this, as if led by electronic versions of Scrooge's ghostly visitors, we were taken to see various examples of church social work and what the video called *education.* Many scenes of old folk being served with well-stocked plates of food. Young children in Christian education *a la Sesame Street.* And so on...and so on. I didn't expect that the trendy video would be full of exquisite Choral Matins from the *BCP* or a William Byrd setting of the Mass. But the fact that there wasn't even a mention, a trace, of such things was a disgrace. The message was: *OK we don't want to have anything to do with the tradition.* But the buzz word of these ecclesiastical trendies is *inclusivity.* So why do they always exclude only the best?

The truth is that the modern worship being put before us both in All Souls' and on the awful video is not truly modern at all: it is only a third rate echo of recently abandoned fashions in pop culture. Today's church always follows fashion only, like a Prince Consort, at least one dutiful step behind. I couldn't believe the *Gradual Psalm.* A female singer stood on the rostrum and crooned verses after which we all crooned back the syrupy chorus beginning, *Remember, remember....* Interminable. As the kids say, *Boring.* Without spiritual, intellectual or musical value. *Remember, remember,* What? I could only think, *The fifth of November.* But Oh for a barrel of gunpowder to see off this lot!

We sat through prayers *for those who work in race relations...between communities...who seek to bring signs of enrichment.* What does this psychobabble mean? We experienced the spiritual rape which always follows the utterance of those misleading words, *Let us offer one another a sign of peace...* In his sermon the Bishop said, *Our sociability should not of course be of the superficial back-slapping kind.* It isn't even that, Bishop: it's of the bum-clenchingly embarrassing kind. The Bishop also said, *The assumption that we can consolidate and expand through an appeal to dormant Christian memories is untenable in the face of the millions who have not had the opportunity to acquire the grammar of the Christian faith.* You felt like standing up and asking, *And who's fault's that then?*

I don't know what the service was for. At the climax, the bishops simply consecrated a lot of water. They didn't sprinkle us with it or wash the windows. They just left it there in a receptacle at the front. On second thoughts, it turned out to have accidental or perhaps even providential significance. It was, after all, Epiphany, water into wine. Here we had the perfect emblem of the modernised church: no wine, just water.

That fiasco in All Souls Langham Place was not a rare event. There are atrocities like it taking place in the Church of England every day. For example, on 11th September 2001 I was in Oxford at a clergy conference — a three-line whip for all priests in the City of London Deanery. It was 11am, three hours before the terrible events in New York. We were assembled for worship in the beautiful medieval church of Holy Cross, just behind Merton's playing fields. How might morning prayer have been ordered for this meeting of spiritual professionals, priests, supposedly mature Christians with authority to preach and teach? A dignified and thoroughly Anglican celebration of Holy Communion according to the *BCP* perhaps? Of course not. The *BCP* is *never* used at official Deanery and Diocesan gatherings of the clergy.

As the early autumn sun lit the gothic interior, highlighting the burnished mahogany colours of the pews, the music started: an out-of-tune piano which was itself out-of-tune with an accidental oboe; a violin that sounded like a cat crying because someone had spilt hot milk on its private parts; and a modern clergyman. I knew he was a modern clergyman only because he was wielding a guitar.

We sang banal and meaningless choruses to plinky-plonky music of the "Jesus goes to Toytown" variety. Then we sat through an horrific sermon. The

Bishop of Stepney told us that doctrine doesn't matter: "All you need is love" — tuning us in to the same wavelength as *The Beatles* and reminding me, at least, of the 1960s and the pioneering days of the church's fatuity, the prelude to its intellectual suicide. There is nothing more out of date than an out of date trendy. The Bishop preached one of the most banal and embarrassing sermons I have heard in more than half a lifetime's sojourn in the pews. I feel as if I should caution: "Anyone of a nervous disposition should put this book down *now*."

The Bishop said, "In a few minutes we shall offer one another a sign of peace. I don't want to see handshakes. I want to see you hugging one another. And then I'll tell you something else I want you to do."

The so-called "Peace" was announced and all hell broke loose. Five full minutes of people, grown men and women — priests, for God's sake — wandering around sacred space with great banana-split grins on their faces, proffering more or less sentimental or lewd greetings. When I was sat upon by a vast and enthusiastic lady, I did my customary escape act, fell to my knees and, when she tried to lift me bodily into the furnace of her embrace, exclaimed, "No thank you, madam. I'm English."

Then it was time for the "something else" with which the Bishop of Stepney had threatened us. He bawled out, "I want you to turn to the person next to you, put your hand on his or her shoulders..." ("His or her" — amazing isn't it how political-correctness triumphs over all atrocities?) "...and say three times, 'You are everlastingly loved"

Luckily I found myself not next to the voluminous Deaconess Blenkinsop with the hot lips and fiery breath, but to a pal of mine, the Rector of St James Garlickhythe — the national HQ of The Prayer Book Society. We exchanged quiet promises of a pint come lunchtime. But this was by no means the end of the entertainment. The Bishop went into full pantomime mode. He was almost screaming at us: "That's not enough. Again! Louder!"

And he cocked his hand behind his ear, as Bruce Forsyth used to do all those years ago on *The Generation Game*. I feared this was going to develop. Any minute he might start asking, "Where's the Archdeacon? Has any little boy (or girl) seen the Archdeacon?"

Followed by an hysterical chorus: "He's BEHIND you!"

After that ludicrous service — really a disservice — I had a light lunch and walked into Oxford, bought some books and sat in a little pub off the High over a pint. I returned to my room in college and read for the rest of the afternoon. At six o'clock I went, duty bound, back to church for more of the horrific Noddy liturgy. Only this time the priest — with his shaved head, his designer stubble, leather jacket and lisp — was telling us about the attacks on New York. Then what? Silence maybe? Tears? The General Confession? Not at all. But straight into more of the plinky-plonky, happy-clappy music, and Jesus goes to Toytown again.

The trouble is that this diminished sort of spirituality, this bankrupt, dumbed down, blasphemous style of worship could not do justice to the terrible events that were unfolding across the Atlantic.

And that excitable — "You are everlastingly loved" - bishop is now Archbishop of York.

There are feasts and fasts in all the world's religions. Islam commemorates the weeks of Ramadan each year with due solemnity: extra prayers are said, the people are encouraged to increase and intensify their devotions, and there is a complete fast from all food and drink during the hours of daylight. Ramadan is a moveable season and so in the summer, and especially in northern latitudes, the fast may last for fifteen hours. By this strict devotion, Muslims show that they are serious in the practise of their religion.

Christianity prescribes its own long fasting season: Lent. The six weeks before Easter recall Christ's forty days and forty nights fast in the wilderness when he was tempted by the devil and they culminate in Holy Week, the most sacred season in the Church's Year, when the terrible events of Christ's betrayal, arrest, trial and crucifixion are commemorated in extra services, long Bible readings and prayers. On Maundy Thursday, the day before Good Friday, the church recalls Christ's Last Supper and gives thanks for his institution of the Holy Communion. Clearly, Lent is a most serious season and traditionally it was marked by fasting and extra attendance at church as Christians tried to follow the Way of the Cross.

But in 2007 the Archbishops and Bishops of the Church of England decided that Christians should keep Lent differently. They launched what was billed as *a multimedia campaign* called *Love Life Live Lent* promoted by the Archbishop of Canterbury and the Archbishop of York. They urged all churchpeople to text the word *Lent* to phone number 64343 *to begin receiving suggestions for action* during Lent. As soon as I'd read the details of this jape I felt myself turning queasy.

The justification for the stunt was provided by the noted intellect — "You are everlastingly loved" - the Archbishop of York who informed us that:

"Recent research has shown that generosity is a key ingredient in making neighbourhoods flourish."

Well, it sure beats going round and smacking your neighbours across the face. But do let's congratulate the Archbishop on the quality of this insight. Did we need *research* to tell us this? Who paid for the research? The Church?

What we were supposed to do in this jolly wheeze was to send off for booklets with a smiling orange on the front. There is a children's version and there is an adult version — which gave pause for thought. And in these booklets we were given spiritual things to do in the great penitential season of Lent. These spiritual things include: *Go to a party...Leave a coin in a shopping trolley...Make someone laugh...Have a meat-free day...Wear a smile....Share a treat...Give someone a hug.*

I have one or two questions. Why should a Christian leave a coin in a trolley? The next user might be Mohammad Al Fayed or Victoria Beckham. *Give someone a hug?* What, when the Church had just issued a code of conduct for clergy which says we shouldn't lay hands on anyone? *Make someone laugh?* I know how to do that: ask him to phone a bishop. But it is no laughing matter.

By such glossy, trashy gimmicks we see the abyss into which the mind of the Church has descended. It is a mixture of greetings card sentimentality, cheap advertising cliché with a slice of environmentalism and vegetarianism. Nothing to do with Lent. Nothing to do with the Christian faith at all. It actually emasculates the faith and undermines the Church by camouflaging them as something else, something alien. It amounts to an act of unfaithfulness to Jesus Christ who never hinted that he wished his Church to pervert its true identity in this way.

The worst of it is that no one forced the Church to commit such an act of betrayal. The Church itself decided to go in for this blasphemous pantomime — just as it has in the past decided to throw out its best Bible and its best Prayer Book, to conspire with the new sexual ethics and to hitch its wagon to every passing enthusiasm from CND to climate change. As if the Church of Christ did not have enemies enough without shooting itself so repeatedly in the foot.

What must devout Muslims think of all this as they emerge from Ramadan?

But in the daily life of the Church of England there is always a rash of laughable insanities — though you hardly know whether to laugh or cry. Truro cathedral is the latest to re-invent itself as an all-singing, all-dancing rock 'n' roll music hall. Evensong was not bringing them in, so they decided to import an Elvis impersonator instead. The Dean said the service would "...examine the spiritual side of Elvis." That should take about two seconds. Then what? The rationale for such blasphemous idiocy is that it will bring people to church. Well, I dare say I could fill the church if I provided free beer and 24/7 football on the big screen. But again, what would be the point of that?

Simply getting people into Church is no good unless what they get when they're in there is the Gospel.

I wonder if autumn is the silly season for The Church of England? In October 2006, the Bishop of London, the Archdeacon and I were in bed in France — not the same bed you understand, but adjacent. This was for a clergy conference in Merville in the old seminary now the conference centre for the diocese of Lille. I was asleep at one o'clock in the morning when the alarm went and voices shouting, "There's a fire. Get out! Get out!"

Blearily, I got half-dressed and opened the door. The corridor was filled with smoke. I ran down the three flights of steps and joined the others on the lawn. Five minutes later the French equivalent of the Trumptonshire fire engine arrived and a wholesale conflagration was averted.

In his talk to the conference, Richard Chartres told us what had happened. He said it was a good job he was a vigilant bishop and only half asleep, or he would not have noticed the smoke pouring from a cupboard in the corner of his room. He got out of bed and saw that this cupboard containing the water heater was ablaze and sounded the alarm. He spoke apocalyptically of *the fire in the closet*.

The conference was about urban ministry, and the main part of the discussion was on the church's response to terrorist atrocities, such as happened in London in 2005 when all the City clergy were deployed at the scenes of the explosions. And we also talked about the possibility of interfaith dialogue. Some American clergy involved in the 9/11 attack on New York told us of their experience. And they handed out a glossy brochure they had produced called *New York Disaster Interfaith Services*.

Here we learnt a whole new vocabulary of *unmet needs roundtables; mapped vulnerabilities; networking to convene leadership and facilitate the delivery of services to underserved victims and impacted communities*. I tell you, if Osama bin Laden were susceptible to volleys of bureaucratic jargon, he would be a dead duck by now.

But all the time I was reading this stuff, I kept thinking of the fire in the closet.

It was all jargon. Even in the loo, in French. You stand there and read the notice that says *Ne pas oublier d'appuyer sur le bouton ci-dessous afin d'actioner la chasse d'eau.* Or, as we say in English, *Flush!* A German spoke for an hour like Professor Teufelsdroch and actually said *Twenty-thirdly.* Then one of the Americans spoke for the next hour, telling us that the chief sins in America are *poverty, racism and sexism.* I confess I still don't understand how these can be described as sins instead of as consequences. He told us merrily that the American clergy were trained in *multiple sensitivity and sexual identity.* Obviously, this *multiple sensitivity* did not include sensitivity to the English language. He ended by telling us *I have learnt to be myself.* And I wondered what was the point of that.

Not to be outdone by mere foreigners, the English clergy soon demonstrated that we are not easily surpassed in the matter of jargon. We were told all about how to *energise, enable* through *models* to deal with *bereavement issues* by means of *paradigms, objectives, systems, methodology, diversity, dissemination* and of course *sharing with you.* One priest admitted shamefacedly *I am not a qualified counsellor* — which made me wonder what his theological training had been all about. You wanted to escape to the chapel and say your prayers. But, as usual, the worship was the worst of it.

One priest began the prayers by saying, "Let us pray around the theme of hate. Think of a person in your parish whom you hate. Perhaps you hate yourself? Or you hate God?"

In the debased canticles we changed "forefathers" into "ancestors" — as if ancestor worship were the coming thing in the C. of E. There were huge dollops of touchy-feely and the explicit hatred of tradition. For instance in the hymn we sang,

"Preaching Christ and not our customs,
Let us build a bridge of care."

See the contempt there for our customs. But what if Christ is mediated precisely *through* our customs?

There were vacuous choruses - the eleven-fold repetition of what was not worth singing once. All to dreamily mothballed tunes of the Joan Baez version of 1960s nostalgia. Pools of sentimentality. And then the feminisation of the church which has followed so swiftly on women's ordination: we prayed to the Holy Ghost as "Tender sister." The climax was an act of such stultifying banality that it made you wish you hadn't come. It was called *the symbolic response.*

We each had to leave our pews and be given a little night-light style candle and put them on the floor of the chapel to form the shape of the Cross. All the time the creepy goo of the chorus droning on and on. Grown men, priests, shuffling themselves into this mullarkey. It reminded me of children's television and I wondered whether we were going to be shown how to make an Archdeacon out of egg boxes. And always at the back of my mind was the fire in the closet.

Of course when we went back into the conference sessions I knew what the fire in the closet really is: the ineptitude and faithlessness of the Church in the face of the secularisation of Europe, of our own country in particular. There are prophets in this wasteland. Marcello Pera, the President of the Italian Senate says this:

"A foul wind is blowing through Europe. This same wind blew through Munich in 1938. While the wind might sound like a sigh of relief, it is really a shortness of breath. It could turn out to be the death rattle of a continent that no longer understands what principles to believe and consequently mixes everything together in a rhetorical hodgepodge."

He suggests the only remedy:

"Will the Church, the clergy and the faithful be able to and want to be purified of the relativism that has almost erased their identity and weakened their message and witness?"

There is not much time left. There is a fire in the closet.

Is Rome a better option?

My main concern, as an Anglican priest, is with the Church of England into which I was ordained thirty-seven years ago. But it should not go un-remarked that the Roman Catholic Church long since embarked on a similar programme of iconoclasm perhaps even more destructive than that of the Church of England. For the Catholic Church — "catholic" means "universal" — possessed among its many treasures the pearl of great price: the Mass in Latin, the same service at which Catholics worshipped the world over. In France or Spain, in Australia or Tanganyika, in the USA or Brazil, it was the Latin Mass. Imagine how such ease of communication would be prized by any commercial company or international body such as the United Nations: no need for translations with all their ambiguity, clumsiness and expense. Many people united by a common liturgical language.

In the 1960s, following the Second Vatican Council, the Roman Catholic Church banned the Latin Mass. It was an act of self-immolation so injurious that you could only imagine it as the work of the enemy, the devil. In place of a universal linguistic understanding penetrated deep into the hearts, minds, souls and unconsciousness of Catholics everywhere, there was suddenly a thousand vernaculars. It was the biggest disaster in human communication since the Tower of Babel, made even worse by the tawdry and banal new vernacular forms.

Belatedly, the Roman Catholic Church has realised its mistake. Pope Benedict XVI, writing in the Foreword to *The Reform of the Roman Liturgy* by Klaus Gamber, says:

"What happened after the Council was something else entirely: in the place of liturgy as the fruit of development came fabricated liturgy. We abandoned the organic living process of growth and development over centuries and replaced it — as in a manufacturing process — with a fabrication, a banal, on-the-spot product".

Benedict XVI has recently issued an encyclical calling for the restoration of dignity and beauty in the Mass, for the return of Latin, for the Gregorian chant. Naturally, the English Catholic bishops hate everything in it.

The ecclesiastical totalitarians

What the modernisers steadfastly will not face is the fact that where the old services are used, there the congregations have not declined. This goes for Anglican parishes using the *BCP* or RC churches where the Latin Mass is celebrated. The Eastern Orthodox have hardly changed their liturgy since AD 1254, and they are full for every service. The hierarchy dismisses these awkward facts as "mere populism" – "populism" being the word of choice for totalitarians faced with a stubborn outbreak of democracy.

An especially cruel irony is that the modernising party has hijacked the word "liberal" and attached it to themselves. Nothing could be further from the truth. For they are not liberal. They are vicious authoritarians who have spent these last fifty years imposing their sectarian whims on the parishes, pushing through their secular agenda often by unscrupulous political chicanery, and persecuting clergy and churchwardens who stand up to them. The hierarchy does this mischief chiefly by refusing to appoint to traditional parishes parsons who will uphold *The Book of Common Prayer.* There are numerous example of how this malevolence works in practice.

A long-serving Incumbent of a *BCP* parish eventually retires or dies. The churchwardens fill in all the forms required of them by the central bureaucracy to indicate the sort of priest they would like as the retired priest's successor. They say they want someone who will conduct services in the style to which they have been historically accustomed: from *The Authorised Version* of the Bible and *The Book of Common Prayer.* The hierarchy pretends to take note of this desire. Their tactic is to leave the parish without an Incumbent for many months, claiming that they cannot find a priest who will use the traditional books. After perhaps eighteen months or two years, the lay officers of that parish are worn out with the burden of trying to find a *locum tenens* to officiate at the services each week and to conduct weddings and funerals and so they give in and accept the modernising Vicar thrust upon them by the hierarchy.

There are other and worse betrayals. The bishop's appointments committee will find a replacement candidate who will actually promise to use the traditional books — only when he or she comes in, he will bring in the new services straight away. Or he will say that new services are to be adopted "for an experimental period". It turns out of course to be an experiment without end. Or he will use the new rites for the main Sunday service and, as a sop to the unreconstructed traditionalists — "the diehards and old fogeys" as he calls them — offer Holy Communion (said) — i.e. rushed and mumbled uncomprehendingly at 8am or, as one aggrieved parishioner reported to me, only half joking, "...at seven o'clock in the morning on the fifth Wednesday after Pancake Tuesday". The fact that most of today's clergy do not understand the *AV* or the *BCP* is only to be expected, given that these historic books are not taught in the theological colleges. It is as if the teaching of maths should proceed without reference to the discoveries of Euclid and Pythagoras.

The hierarchy justifies its broken promises and lies by recourse to the timeless deceit of all utilitarians: "It's for their own good in the long run."

When I speak about some of these goings-on in the contemporary church, many people suggest to me that perhaps I am laying it on a bit thick, that I am exaggerating the travesties. Far from it. If anything, I am understating the noxious behaviour that happens daily. Try to imagine the most outrageous desecration possible and you will find you have underestimated the crassness of the church hierarchy.

Richard Harries, the recently retired Bishop of Oxford, has cautioned churchpeople about the language used by the priest at Mass. He wrote: "People who are groping their way into Christianity can suddenly find themselves shocked and horrified at the sacrificial, cannibalistic language of the Eucharist. Christians do not take seriously enough people's sense of horror at going to a Eucharist or Mass and hearing the imagery of sacrifice and eating God". He said we should not use those words given and commanded us by Jesus Christ, "Take, eat, this is my Body...this is my Blood" and recommends that we use expressions such as "the food of angels" and "the bread of life" instead. When one of the most senior bishops in the land says such things, what words are left to describe his blasphemous dereliction?

In summary, the modernisers do not believe in the traditional doctrines, they do not uphold traditional morality and they have thrown out the traditional Scripture and liturgies. They have nothing in common with traditional believers, with the forms and phrases in which Christianity has been expressed and practised in our nation for a millennium. They are another sort of church altogether — a church that does not fight "against the world, the flesh and the devil" but which accommodates all three in its capitulation to secular modernity.

III: Some jokes are no laughing matter

Poisonous Political-Correctness

We all have our favourite jokes about Political-Correctness, whether it is the urban legend about the banning of black bin-bags because they were considered "racist" or Ann Widdecombe's riposte to a BBC producer who described her as "Chair". I am a Chairman, not a chair – I have never been sat upon!"

Most people regard Political-Correctness as a bit of a joke and a bit of a laugh, but in its serious consequences it is neither. Consider one of the most far-reaching consequences of PC in recent times: the Macpherson Enquiry which followed the murder of Stephen Lawrence. This is the enquiry which invented the ill-defined concepts "institutional racism" and "unconscious racism" and declared the police force to be institutionally racist. When sceptics asked for a justification for these tendentious neologisms, Lord Macpherson declared loftily,

"We do not pretend to produce a definition which will carry all argument before it".

In other words, we won't answer your awkward questions. Just like the secret police.

Worse, the MacPherson Enquiry went on to define a racist incident as:

"An incident so described by the victim, *or any other person*".

This too is meaningless of course, but it is the catch-all, you're-guilty-even-when-you're-innocent terminology of the gulag. If *anything* can be legitimately described as a racist incident, then when I ask you if you'd like a cup of tea, you can report me to the race relations authorities. Meaningless jargon, politically-correct or not, is not merely spurious: when a meaningless expression is made the basis of a law of the land it is a prescription for confusion and chaos. Certainly the definition of a racist incident set out by Macpherson is incoherent and as such cannot reasonably stand as the basis for law-making. But it does and so makes us all victims of an insane procedure. Badly-framed legal definitions damage our whole society and undermine our way of life.

Among those who dared criticise the Macpherson Report, William Hague, former Leader of Her Majesty's Opposition, said:

"It has led to every police officer in Britain being branded a racist." Hague promised to "...take on and defeat the liberal elite that has never trusted the police force and now wants us to believe they are all racists".

There is racial prejudice in Britain today, but is it as widespread and ingrained as the race-relations industry makes out? "Institutional racism" is a systematically vague expression. It is relatively easy to demonstrate racial prejudice in an individual, but how would you go about showing that a whole institution such as the police force or, as Archbishop Sentamu has said, The Church of England, is guilty of this crime?

And the PC obsession with race leads to some bizarre consequences: for example, murder is bad — or as Orwell, who understood the lying manipulation of language for political purposes better than anyone, defined it "doubleplusungood". But "racially-aggravated murder" is worse and actually attracts a more severe sentence. I wonder if the worst suffering of the victim of a drive-by-shooting as he lies in a pool of his own blood is the echo of his assailant's insult, "White bastard!" Bizarrely, racially aggravated murder is one of those events which comes under the category of "hate crime" — as if other criminal acts were perpetrated out of affection and love. It is this sort of example which conclusively demonstrates the absurdity of PC.

The PC category of racism does not allow us to speak the truth. If you say, rightly, that black athletes on the whole run faster than white athletes, that is acceptable. But if you say that ninety per cent of the gun crime in Britain is perpetrated by black men, you will be in trouble. It is facts like these which demonstrate the socially-destructive power of PC — for no society can be secure when it deliberately and constantly misleads itself about what is actually going on in that society.

Lies are the original house built on sand. And the house built on sand cannot endure when the rough weather comes. Of course we have free speech in this country — it's just that we're not allowed to say things that are officially disapproved. "Democracy" was once cynically defined as "Say what you like but do what you're told". Now even the saying is banned. As I write, David Coleman, Professor of Demography at Oxford, is being hounded because he has ventured to criticise the PC line on immigration — that it is always beneficial to this country and a fine thing, above criticism. Professor Coleman said:

"It seems to me to lead to the creation of an establishment consensus in the respectable media and elsewhere, intolerant of dissenting interpretations, regarding them as almost axiomatically to be heretical or malevolent."

My only question to Professor Coleman is to ask him why he thought the "almost" to be necessary in that sentence. Professor Coleman does not deny that much immigration is beneficial: he is merely questioning whether *all* immigration is beneficial. And for this he is pilloried. Not only does PC not allow us to state the truth concerning many social issues, but it does not even allow us to *ask* what the truth might be in a particular case. This is totalitarianism and it is operated according to the apparatus of PC: the control of our thoughts and speech by an establishment elite. To say this is not exaggeration, scare-mongering or ranting. There are many instances, such as the one featuring Professor Coleman, in which dissidents from the PC line are gagged, shouted down or even prosecuted and forced out of their jobs.

In the dogmatic system of PC, racism has a twin called "sexism". This is an artificial construct which at some time in the 1960s and 1970s began to replace chivalry and good manners in the definition of attitudes towards women. No one denies that the emancipation of women was and is a good thing, but political and social emancipation were only interim goals for the PC feminists. They demand absolute equality. But this is logically impossible, for equality can only be between things that are alike. And we have noticed that, while men and women share a common humanity, they are not alike in certain crucial respects.

Women are made for childbearing. Why should it be contentious to say this? It is just a fact of life. And with childbearing comes child-rearing — a task which traditionally belongs more to the woman than to the man. The reason for this is not that every civilisation known to history has deliberately sought to imprison women in the home: it is because women are naturally suited to child-rearing — which is not to say that men may not play their part in this activity.

I have defended women as child-bearers and child-raisers on ontological grounds, and of course I accept the fact that not everyone will agree with this approach. But even on the practical and utilitarian grounds — so beloved elsewhere by modern moralists — there are good reasons for thinking that absolute equality of function between men and women in the running of the family is not a good thing. It is an idealist's dream that a woman with two children under the age of four should be free to leave the family and join the army — or even set herself up as a full time member of a peace-movement. There are practical consequences if she does. Someone else — another woman? - has to be engaged to look after the children. Besides, is it best for the well-being of the family if mothers and children are separated and surrogates are brought in? Perhaps it is. But that is not the point: the point is that PC does not even allow us to ask this sensible question. Because PC is not a range of policies developed in response to circumstances: it is an ideology, a prejudice. And even — especially — a society based on utilitarian principles should take account of the facts.

PC is sometimes taken to be simply the codification of modern manners. The world has changed and sensitivities have become more refined. We are said to have "moved on." So, for example, attitudes and conduct which would have passed without comment a generation ago are now rightly outlawed as offensive to women, for instance, or to ethnic minorities. This programme is presented as modern, liberated and high-minded, but in reality it is something else entirely, something nasty and subversive of our established way of life.

Wittgenstein said, "Change a language and you change a world". And this is what PC has achieved. It has done so in the manner predicted by George Orwell in his novel *1984* — that is by abolishing disapproved words so that they become literally *unthinkable* while a list of approved neologisms becomes compulsory. PC is not innocent, neutral and fair-minded. It is a way of banishing dissent, made all the worse by the pretence to be doing this out of fair-minded and "liberating" motivation. In short, PC is a form of linguistic dictatorship and social conditioning — made more dangerous by its subtlety, its appeal to our better nature and the admonition that it is all being done for our own good. You might call PC "dictatorship-lite". I will give some examples of its perniciousness.

There are many aspects of PC which appear benign, even enlightened. Who, for example, could object to the coining of more kindly expressions to refer to people who suffer physical and mental adversity? So in the modern world there are no blind people, nor deaf nor intellectually retarded — only the partially-sighted, the hearing-impaired and those with learning difficulties. There are mildly amusing unintended consequences of these innovations. For they change our traditional and conversational language of simile and metaphor: you can't really say, "As partially-sighted as a bat"; "As hearing-impaired as a post"; and "With the learning difficulties of three short planks".

It may be argued that this impoverishment of common speech is more than made up for by the more enlightened and humane new references to those who are physically or mentally disabled. But euphemisms rarely do any good, for they gloss over what is hard and cruel with the result that the weasel words prevent us from seeing the harsh aspects of the world as they really are. You would be inclined to have more sympathy for a man described as "blind" rather than one who is *only* "partially-sighted" – which doesn't sound so bad. Our deepest pity needs to be stirred if we are to go to the aid of an injured, disabled or poverty-stricken person. But it is precisely our pity which is undermined by weasel words and phrases which imply that the actual suffering is not so very severe. So when PC enthusiasts declare that their euphemistic neologisms are the way to create "a more compassionate society", their method is in opposition to their stated aim.

And sometimes PC euphemisms go so far as to destroy meaning altogether – as we saw in the case of The Macpherson Report. For instance, once there were some people who were "poor". But "poor" sounds derogatory or patronising, so now there are no poor but only "underprivileged". This is nonsensical, for it implies that – after the banning of "poor" – there are only left to us various degrees of "privilege", the "underprivileged", the "overprivileged" and the rest who, we are obliged to conclude, are merely "privileged". This is to render language meaningless. And to do this is not a small matter.

Anyone reading the great reforming political philosophers of the 18th and 19th centuries would infer from their works that "toleration" is a good word, standing as it does for a quality of generosity to be sought after. Surely we *ought* to be tolerant? And so we tried to be until the coming of PC when "toleration" became a dirty word. For now, unlike in the days of John Stuart Mill, to tolerate an activity implies that the one who does the tolerating is in a superior moral or social position from which he is prepared graciously to put up with aberrations of various sorts. And of course, for the devotees of PC, there is no such position. There is not even such a status as "normal" – for the very ascription of the word "normal" is alleged to insult all who do not share the so-called "normal" attributes or proclivities. And this just means that we can no longer use the word "normal" coherently. Destroy a language and you destroy a world. According to PC, homosexuality is as normal as heterosexuality. You begin to wonder what precisely are the strictures which would render paedophilia or necrophilia "abnormal". There is no longer "perversity", only "diversity". So many moral (qualitative) concepts are reduced to being merely functional descriptions (quantitative).

Because words have meanings, they have political and social consequences of the most far-reaching kind. Take the word "ghetto" for instance. This conjures up unpleasant recollections of the Second World War and the Warsaw Ghetto in which many Polish people suffered and died under the Nazis. So no one of good will would wish to create new ghettos. So let's use a nice word such as "community" instead. Now "community" means all of us, the whole people. But that is not how it is used now under PC. Instead we have the Muslim community, the Jewish community, the Gay community. Hilariously, *The Independent* newspaper once referred to "London's sadomasochistic community". So according to PC, "community" now means "group" or "sect". By changing the meaning of the word, PC is creating sectarianism — ghettos which, it was alleged, no one wants.

One of the most prized qualities of humankind is the ability to discern, to make judgements and to value one thing above another thing. PC condemns this intelligent, sensitive capacity as being "judgemental". And "discrimination", while it used to mean the refined ability to differentiate between one thing and another, is now only used in a pejorative sense: it is a dirty word. Indeed, PC does not allow us to claim that one thing is better than another — that, say, the music of Bach is rather better than that of Sid Filth and the Stranglers. For that would be an example of "elitism". But to teach discrimination is surely the aim of education. Thus education is undermined altogether by PC. Why should the devoted teacher labour to inculcate notions of quality and to lure his charges into making subtle moral and aesthetic judgements if one thing is as good as another? So PC does not allow us to talk about "value". We might ask, incidentally, whether, if we are not allowed to be elitists, we should aspire to become mediocritists.

A.J. Ayer and the emotivist philosophers of the 1930s divided evaluative words into two classes: words of approbation and words of disapproval — "Hurrah!" or "Boo!" as they said. Today we have words which are used in these emotive senses but without rational justification. So, someone who walks along to Trafalgar Square among a lot of other people carrying banners and shouting slogans may be called a member of the "peace-movement". Or the same man might take himself off to a war zone such as Iraq or Afghanistan and hinder the troops, where he might be captured by the enemy and cause "a hostage crisis" — a situation beloved of the mass media but which only makes difficulties for the British government and possibly involves our troops in a dangerous rescue mission.

What has that man done for peace? His march to Trafalgar Square carrying a ban-the-bomb banner is done in support of the policy of unilateral nuclear disarmament. But what if our unilateralism makes us more vulnerable to an enemy nuclear attack? After all there is a precedent: the only nation to suffer a nuclear attack were the Japanese, and they did not have nuclear weapons with which to threaten a response. It is not self-evident that pacifism produces peace; in fact the historical evidence may tell convincingly against that view. But PC guarantees that nothing must stop the pacifist unilateralist with his banner and his nuisance-value being accorded the accolade as a member of the "peace movement". "Peace movement" is simply a "Hurrah!" word without rational or empirical connotation, and so just as emotive as any category dreamed up by Ayer and his colleagues in the 1930s. Perhaps often the most effective peacemakers are soldiers. And it is impossible to hold a sensible conversation — let alone devise a national defence policy — on the basis of merely emotive slogans.

The opposition between "Hurrah!" and "Boo!" is the basic linguistic-emotive apparatus by which the world is redefined according to the new canons of PC. Two "Boo!" words with very far reaching consequences for political conversation are "nationalism" and "imperialism". Even those clever people who do all the interviews on such as *The Today Programme* are not quite clever enough to see that these are words which come with ideological weighting. They are theory-laden. This baggage goes all un-remarked, if not unnoticed. It is simply unconsciously assumed that nationalism and imperialism are bad things.

Let us concede that they might indeed be bad things. The point is though that the examination of whether they are good or bad, desirable or undesirable, is never made. But, as Socrates said, "The unexamined life is not worth living". Whereas, you might think it is the duty of the public's grand inquisitors on the broadcast media to look deeper than clichéd definitions and verbal prejudices. Bad things have been done in the name of the nation, but many good results have been achieved to be set alongside the bad. Are we to suppose that the inquisitors have done their utilitarian calculus and come to the view that the bad so eclipses the good that we can confidently assume that nationalism is, always and everywhere and in every respect, undesirable? If the sums have been done, I should like very much to see evidence of the working.

Isn't it a mark of the unbiased intelligence that we should observe these arguments being evaluated? Unbiased intelligence is not much in evidence on the BBC. And when it comes to "imperialism", the boos get even louder. No current affairs commentator on radio or television asks of any empire, "Was it a good empire?" *All* imperialism is the mark of the beast. And so it might be. Again, that is not the point. The point is simply that the question should be raised and discussion joined: what, for example, did the Roman Empire ever do for us? Some might say it did quite a lot.

And this is the debilitating character of PC: it is anti-intellectual, unreasonable, illogical and non-empirical. It does not examine the facts before coming to a judgement. It has already come to its judgements, and in the light of these judgements it redefines the facts. That is what is meant by an ideology. If everyone has his umbrella up and his raincoat on in Moscow and people everywhere are scurrying into doorways, we might infer that it is raining. But under the discipline of dialectical materialism, which for so long held sway in that city, they decided whether it was raining or not by (so to speak) consulting the government's weather forecast in *Pravda*. Mere facts must not be allowed to get in the way of accepted prejudice. And that is the hallmark of PC.

Once you get into the habit of talking about nationalism and imperialism, you must get into the other habit of apologising for the past: for Britain was a nation state with an imperialistic history. It follows that we must have done many terrible things: in fact, given the "Boo!" status of "nationalism" and "imperialism", almost everything we have done needs to be apologised for. How far are we to take this duty to apologise, and does it apply to all nations, not just the unspeakably imperial Brits? Should the Muslims, as well as ourselves, say sorry for their part in the Crusades, the Russians for invading Czechoslovakia and Italian ice cream men for the sins, negligences and ignorances of the Roman Empire?

Besides, a great deal of this apologising is misplaced. We have just lived through a Schmaltzfest of apologising for the slave trade — as if the slave trade had ended as recently as last year. The truth is that the slave trade was abolished two hundred years ago *and it was we who abolished it.* Therefore, any recollection of the slave trade on the 200th anniversary of our abolishing it ought to have taken the form not of an apology but a celebration and thanksgiving for, let it be said, the Christian gentlemen who abolished it: *that* despised class of non-PC "reactionaries".

It is ironical that the PC generation which does not believe in *personal* guilt — every man responsible for his own sins — yet makes us all share a *corporate* guilt which has no cause in fact and therefore for which confession makes no logical sense. This illogical view of moral responsibility permeates the whole of life after PC. So, for instance, I am fat not because I eat too much and take no exercise: I am only "suffering from" obesity. It is suggested that my fatness is not my responsibility — though of course I must be called to account for the bombing of Dresden which happened before I was born.

The world of medicine, and especially of psychology and psychiatry, has been redesigned according to the canons of PC. There are PC ailments and diseases. In 2005 a man aged eighteen murdered his parents, took their credit cards and ran off to a posh hotel in New York with his girlfriend. When his case eventually came to court, he was acquitted of murder because it was said he was "suffering from Narcissistic Personality Disorder". What's the difference between NPD and being a scheming murderer? In this way, PC removes all occasions for justifiable personal guilt and tries to inculcate a spurious corporate guilt over matters concerning which we could never have had any influence.

PC ruins our institutions by making them subject to policies which destroy their original character and purpose. And it characteristically achieves this by the invention of new modes of approbation. Consider higher education and the university. Totalitarian egalitarianism has decided that these institutions should be made "accessible" and promote "inclusivity". But the university was always accessible, provided you were clever enough to pass the entrance examinations. There was a class of person described as "university standard". That would not do for the PC revolutionaries: all shall run and all shall win glittering prizes.

So the standards were lowered and the university courses democratised and dumbed down beyond recognition. Anyone comparing the "A" level papers of today with those set forty years ago will see at once what a falling off there has been. And, when the entrant gains his place in the university, it might be to study Fashion and Hairdressing or Golf Studies with Ten Pin Bowling. There is nothing wrong with Fashion, Hairdressing, Golf or Ten Pin Bowling. Anyone might practise them with profit. They are just not pastimes which belong in the university. By making them part of a university education, the PC levellers have set these leisure subjects on the same level as Classics and Pure Mathematics. When the criteria for discrimination are removed like this, the destruction of the whole idea and reality of the university is guaranteed. For the idea of the university is of a place of discrimination and excellence. Unfortunately, PC annihilates both.

The technique of the PC enthusiasts is like that of the Greeks who insinuated themselves into Troy by means of the wooden horse: something that looks nice and friendly turns out to contain a nasty surprise. For example, no decent human being could be against provision for disabled people and for taking

81

sensible precautions according to the wider definitions of "health and safety". But even benefits are turned into deficits under the rule of PC.

Many potentially beneficial projects become undermined and even cancelled when it becomes obvious that an organisation cannot afford to pay the full cost of provision for the disabled. I know this from experience. I am Rector of a church in the City where we are fortunate to enjoy the charity of the Corporation of London which provided for the installation of our "disabled loo" and a wheelchair-ramp. But not all parishes, nor other organisations, are so fortunate and so frequently we hear of an innovative project — such as an extension to provide kitchens and leisure facilities — becoming stymied because its proposers cannot afford to pay for the exact provision stipulated.

And so the greater good of the greater number is thwarted in the interests not even of the minority but in the interests of the bossy PC bureaucracy which insists there is only one way to fulfil the community's obligations to the disabled. Often there are more informal ways of getting disabled people in and out — what did we ever do before there was PC? — but these are not regarded as satisfactory by the apparatchiks who make the rules. How ever did Douglas Bader manage, we wonder, without a disabled ramp for his Spitfire?

Similarly, we read every autumn of headteachers who ban conkers — along with swings and slides in the playground and school trips into the countryside for fear that some child will fall into the river. This particular example indicates very clearly what precisely is wrong at the root of PC: it does not respond to the world as it is but to an idealised view of the world in which no one ever slips on the ice or falls out of a swing or drowns. But unfortunately the world is so ordered that every year a few people will drown: the many will not. PC regulations mean once more that the exceeding benefits of any activity must be forfeited in the face of some minute risk. The impression is undeniable that the devotees of PC would do away with the law of gravity if they could, since it is responsible for monkeys falling out of trees.

The way in which health and safety regulations and the fantasy which is the PC understanding of human rights intrudes into public life may finally result in truly disastrous consequences. Many commentators and specialists in military affairs are currently warning that the PC obsession with these regulations and imagined rights is ruining the training of our armed forces. At the time of the capture of fifteen British sailors and marines by Iranian pirates in the Gulf, I made a feeble joke which turned out to be an accurate prophecy. I said, "The sailor taken into solitary confinement probably missed most his I-pod." Only later I discovered that that sailor had actually worn his I-pod while boarding ships suspected of carrying contraband.

Every civilisation, and even every period in the development of a civilisation is ultimately based on a deep sense or feeling of how things ought to be. Every civilisation has its codes and laws of course; but this sense or feeling is deeper and is usually based on an absolute presupposition which gives rise to or generates the codes and laws. Such a presupposition might be, for example, a belief in God. It doesn't have to be this belief: it could be another profound influence altogether — such as that we should live so as to please the departed spirits of our ancestors. The fundamental presupposition, whatever it is, is not usually questioned, except by a few scholars. And why should it be? People have better things to do — such as getting on with living their lives. Truly, the unexamined life is not worth living; but it is possible to examine one's life to death.

But it is important to understand that the fundamental, formative presupposition *is* a presupposition: it is something that a civilisation takes for granted. It is akin to the *Zeitgeist* — the spirit of the age. It might be Torah or Catholic Christianity, or in another place the cycle of the Hindu gods and goddesses. The fundamental presuppositions of the present age are progress and modernity. These categories are never questioned, but simply assumed. The result is that, for example, people might question whether a particular activity or policy was really a mark of progress or modernity; but no one questions whether progress and modernity are good in themselves: their rightness and goodness is just assumed, for they are our society's basic presuppositions. And the language which operates and mediates the basic presuppositions of progress and modernity is PC which prescribes which things *cannot be said* and, by extension, which things *cannot be thought.*

There are typical *Zeitgeist* "Hurrah!" and "Boo!" words operated by PC. "Progress" and "modern" — with all their connectives: modernisation, progressed, progressive etc. And prominent among the "Boo!" words is "taboo". Journalism is full of cliches about "the last taboo". A taboo, according to PC modernity, is always regarded as a bad thing and it is entirely overlooked that the purpose of a taboo in the first place was to warn us off certain physically harmful or socially disruptive activities.

But modernity and the progressive attitude was originally fuelled by Freud — particularly by his attack on monotheism *Totem and Taboo* — and his warnings about the danger of "repression" which naturally germinated into the debauched cry of 1960s pop-psychology for us to "let it all hang out". The assumption of course is that taboos were necessary for the poor, ignorant and primitive types who were our forebears, but that our generation has outgrown these foolish superstitions. It is the secular slogan "man come of age" all over again. One can only conjecture whether there will come a time when our society is so gloriously emancipated, modernised and secularised that it will have done away with all taboos: not only incest, which many already think is long overdue for abolition, but the taboos against paedophilia, coprophilia and sadomasochism

Another "Boo!" word is "religion" — especially Christianity and Orthodox Judaism: that is to say, against the adherents of those faiths who actually take their faith seriously enough to believe it. Reformed Jews and "liberal" Christians are acceptable to modernity, because they have accepted the secular canons and made the teachings of their faith subordinate to modernity — actually interpreting their faith as if it were a metaphor for secular nostrums and attitudes.

Thus the Exodus from Egypt led by Moses comes to be seen not as a particular historical act of Divine deliverance, but a sort of abstract example of the notion of freedom in general — freedom from anything: sexual repression, the narrow confines of marriage, the kitchen and of course from all taboos. And Christ's feeding of the five thousand was not a miracle but an injunction to "sharing," to feeding Africa, and generally for us all to reject the various nastinesses of capitalism and the globalised economy. Of course the PC moderns do not pause to ask themselves why any serious Jew or Christian should accept those platitudinous interpretation of Divine intervention as religiously formative. But who would want to build a religious faith on such vapidity?

PC decrees that Islam be exempted from criticism — but it is more likely that it escapes because any opportunistic blasphemer would fear for his life if he insulted the Koran or the Prophet. The way the mass media, with a few brave exceptions, refused to reprint the humorous cartoons of Mohammad was a betrayal of their duty to stand up for free speech — a quality the media is proud to uphold, so long as its upholding does not threaten the interests of the media men themselves. You can occasionally find an exception to the prevailing cowardice. The hilarious and scurrilous satirical comic *Viz* began an item with its cartoon hero saying in his speech-bubble: "I think I'll go down to the mosque and make a few jokes about Islam." In the cartoon's next frame he sensibly changes his mind: "On second thoughts, I think I'll be safer going to the parish church instead!"

As a parish priest, I imbibe more religious broadcasting than the average and, among the many quirks in presentation which I have observed, is one so blatant and recurrent that it has become definitive. Whenever a radio or TV presenter reports on a Muslim festival, he gives the historical origin of the festival in this way: "Today Muslims are commemorating the Ascension of the Prophet, the *Miraj* when Mohammad went up on a staircase to heaven."

But when reporting a Christian festival, there is always the added caveat: "Christians believe" or "For Christians…" For example, "Easter Day when, *according to Christians*, Christ rose from the dead."

The God of the Jews and the Christians is mocked, reviled and blasphemed as a matter of ordinary programming throughout the mass media. There are always plenty of jokes about Jews and circumcision, but you won't hear any jokes about circumcision as practised in the Muslim faith. Recently I heard on a radio "comedy" show an off colour joke about a Rabbi, his shawl and what he did with it in connection with a woman. You won't hear any skits about

85

Muslims sticking their backsides in the air when they pray. Moses and the Ten Commandments are a ripe source of media bawdy, but there are no skits on the Koran. God and Christ are blasphemed routinely, their names and titles used as expletives like *fuck* and *shit*. The name of the Prophet is *never* taken in vain.

BBC executives held a discussion in 2007 about objects which may be "dumped" - thrown away — by participants in the show *Room 101*. It was decreed that it is permissible to dump the Bible but not the Koran. Incidentally, when I type the word "koran" with the "k" in lower case, the spellchecker always "corrects" to the capital letter. There is no such correction made when I type the word "bible" or "gospel"

In 2005 the BBC's broadcasting of *Jerry Springer the Opera* received 47,000 complaints from listeners. This show featured a foul-mouthed, shit-eating Jesus who describes himself as "a bit Gay", constantly insults the Virgin Mary and screams hysterical profanities against the Devil. As Stephen Green, Director of Christian Voice, said at the time: "If *Jerry Springer the Opera* is not blasphemous, then nothing in Britain is sacred." The BBC defended the award-winning — but what could "award" mean here? - production, saying: "We are pleased that a wider audience has been able to see an important piece of contemporary culture."

So now at least we have the definition of *culture* according to the BBC whose Director General declares himself a practising Roman Catholic. But by its consistently offensive treatment of the most revered biblical characters, the BBC demonstrates its secular bias and its hostility towards Christianity and Judaism.

The PC subservience of traditional faith to modern secularism has found many other practical instances. For instance, Health and Safety regulations compel churches to prioritise access for the disabled. We take these regulations very seriously at our church of St Michael's in the City of London, and so we asked our architect to draw up plans for a handrail beside our steep steps. We had the project approved by the Diocese of London and costed. Of course, being naturally compliant in all things, we also took spiritual soundings from the

Diocesan Advisory Committee and we sought the refined aesthetic judgment of the National Council for the Care of Churches. In all these things we were successful and so we came to the point when we needed to pay for the handrail.

There is a charitable institution here called The City Bridge Trust and the Trustees will often pay specifically for disabled access projects. So St Michael's applied. I will not take up pages with the "information package", a foot thick, which they sent in answer to our application; but its main requirements make instructive reading. The Trust might pay for disabled access to a church providing this funding is understood as being used only for secular purposes. So disabled audiences at our Monday organ recitals, City workers come in to eat their luncheon sandwiches and blundering tourists come to gawp at the ceiling are all deemed worthy recipients of the charity of the City Bridge Trust. But the Christians are excluded. In other words, the Trust will give charitable assistance to churches provided that on no account is the money used to ease the passage into church of those who wish to worship God.

The scandal is, of course, that the very idea of charity was originally a religious idea and that organisations such as the City Bridge Trust owe their ethos to the religious commitment of their Founders. But now they have been so captivated by aggressive secularism that they oppose Christianity with all the practical means at their disposal.

My second example is of something more serious and far-reaching because it concerns not just the regulations of a local charity but the law of the land. Churches have historically been regarded as charities in the full legal meaning of that term — which is not remarkable, given the definition of "charity" by that noted Founder of Churches, St Paul in *I Corinthians 13*. But from next year, all churches are to be obliged to register as official charities with the Charities Commission. Churchwardens will have to become Trustees in the meaning of the Act — never mind that the office of churchwarden is one that not only predates the Charities Commission by a millennium but even predates the office of Vicar or Rector.

Moreover, in order to qualify as charities, churches will have to show not only that they "advance religion" — which for centuries has been enshrined in law as a charitable cause — but also that their work "benefits the public." In other words, it is no longer to be assumed that religion is good in itself but it will have to demonstrate an additional sort of benefit; and this when the word "benefit" itself takes its origin from "beneto", be blessed. This imminent legal innovation cannot be understood as anything but a secularising attack on the Christian faith.

By the side of this exclusion from the concepts of charity and benefit, the additional fact that the PC secularisers have also decreed that the Priest must put up "No Smoking" signs in the church porch seems only mildly amusing. This is a redundant gesture if ever there was one, since I have never seen anyone attempt to smoke in church — no, not in thirty-seven years as a priest and ten years as an altar boy before that. Even we altar boys knew better than to light up in the sanctuary!

Where did Political-Correctness Come From?

PC is not an accidental mutation in the development of society and culture: it is a change in what T.S. Eliot called "sensibility", in the unconscious presuppositions which, while they themselves go unexamined, form the mores of culture and society. I believe that PC originated in modern times in the work and ambitions of a radical political group, the Institute for Marxism which became known as the Frankfurt School. Patrick J. Buchanan in his book *The Death of the West* says,

"Political-Correctness is cultural Marxism. In a third of a century, what was denounced as the counterculture has become the dominant culture, and what was the dominant culture has become a dissident culture, an ideological state, a soft tyranny where the new orthodoxy is enforced not by police agents, but by inquisitors of the popular culture".

I would only amend this to include police agents. What else, when the police are called to schools to arrest children for calling one another "racist" names —

as happened in at least one state school in Britain in 2007. In another recent incident, police in London removed the barbed wire which residents had put up over the roof of a block of flats after a series of burglaries: it was to be understood that the barbed wire presented a danger to the burglar in the course of his occupation — as if it were a form of the restriction of trade.

The precursors and originators of the Frankfurt School included Georg Lukacs (1885-1971) who declared, "I saw the revolutionary destruction of society as the one and only solution" — where the solution was the overthrow of Western capitalism. But, as Buchanan, points out, it was not economic capitalism which stood in the way of the revolutionaries' ambitions but the ancient order that underlay it:

"Marx had been wrong. Capitalism was not impoverishing the workers. Indeed their lot was improving and they had not risen in revolution because their souls had been saturated in two thousand years of Christianity. Unless and until Christianity and Western culture, the immune system of capitalism, were uprooted from the soul of Western man, Marxism could not take root. In biblical terms, the word of Marx had fallen on rock-hard Christian soil and died".

Lukacs saw the necessity for the destruction of Christian civilisation and he advocated "demonic ideas" in the spread of "cultural terrorism". It is to Lukacs therefore that I am indebted for the title of this book. Lukacs was Hungarian, an agent of the Comintern and he set up a schools programme in which children were instructed in free love, and sexual intercourse while being taught that the family was an outdated institution along with monogamy and all manifestations of religion. His aim was to undermine the family by promoting licentiousness among women and children and so weaken the basis of Christian living.

Buchanan prophesied accurately the means by which the new order would become established: "Contraception, sterilisation, abortion and euthanasia — the four horsemen of the culture of death."

Another of these cultural revolutionaries and nihilistic iconoclasts was the Italian Communist, Antonio Gramsci (1891-1937) who noticed that the Russian people had not been converted to Communism: rather, they hated it. Gramsci called for "a long march through the institutions" — the arts, the cinema, education, theological seminaries, the mass media and the new medium of radio. Gramsci became fashionable among the *radical chic* revolutionaries of the 1960s and 70s, among them Charles Reich who revealed Gramsci's influence on him in his best-selling, *The Greening of America:*

"There is a revolution coming. It will not be like revolutions of the past. It will originate with the individual and with culture, and it will change the political structure only as its final act. It will not require violence to succeed and it cannot be successfully resisted with violence. It is now spreading with amazing rapidity and already our laws, institutions and social structures are changing in consequence."

Victory in the culture wars was guaranteed once Christianity had died in the soul of Western man. This was happening at a speed which the revolutionaries could hardly have imagined in their most optimistic moments. I described the conflict as "culture wars". In fact there was only a phoney war, as Christian civilisation surrendered as soon as the first shots were fired. The method of the nihilists was an ideology of perpetual change, the human spirit the subject and victim of endless malleability. This method found its rationale in the doctrine of "absolute historicism" — which meant that all morals, values and standards were products of the age. There are no absolute moral standards and morality itself should be seen as something which is "socially constructed".

The leading light — one is tempted to say misleading darkness — of the 1960s revolution was Herbert Marcuse (1898-1979) who invented Critical Theory whose supporters repeated over and again the slogans that Western societies are racist, sexist, xenophobic, homophobic, anti-Semitic, fascist and Nazi. The fundamental ambition of Critical Theory was the mass inculcation of "cultural pessimism" and "alienation" wherein, as Buchanan says, "A people, though prosperous and free, comes to see its society and country as oppressive, evil and unworthy of affection and love."

Marcuse knew that past revolutions had prospered by the use of rallying oratory and persuasive books, but he believed drugs and sex were better weapons. In his book *Eros and Civilisation* he called for the universal embrace of the Pleasure Principle — derived of course from Freud — and the creation of a world of "polymorphous perversity". It was like the trumpet call of the pagans and bacchanalians who stirred the Israelites to the licentiousness of the Golden calf while Moses was up the mountain talking with God. Marcuse's famous slogan caught on worldwide; "Make love, not war."

Marcuse's colleague, Wilhelm Reich produced a hugely successful movie *WR The Mysteries of the Organism* which argued "There is no political revolution without first a sexual revolution". The sexual revolution was simply the abolition of traditional Christian morality and the family.

The western world seemed to be full of antinomian gurus, radical chic professional people who used their respected positions in society to undermine society. These included Timothy Leary (1920-1996), the anti-psychologist who preached the virtues of the psychedelic drug LSD and nihilism:

"My advice to people today is as follows: If you take the game of life seriously, if you take your nervous system seriously, if you take your sense organs seriously, if you take the energy process seriously, you must turn on, tune in, and drop out."

That is to say, life, beyond the pleasure principle, is meaningless.

It was no argument to point to the fact that the Western societies denounced as tyrannical and oppressive by the cultural revolutionaries were actually so free and accommodating that even its declared mortal enemies and those who worked for its destruction were able to speak and write freely.

This was a great success among the student radicals and hippies in Europe and the USA in the 1960s and 70s — a generation privileged and pampered beyond all its predecessors, which came to pity itself as oppressed and downtrodden by "authority." I was an undergraduate at Liverpool University at the time and I remember the sit-ins and trying to find out what these were about. I was told that the students were protesting their sit-ins because "The authorities are keeping secret files on us all."

"How do you know? What evidence have you got?"

"We can't know and there is no evidence available — because the files are secret"

Secret files and non-existent files: the identity of indiscernibles.

Those decades too saw the origin of the therapeutic state, in which sin was redefined as illness, crime was only aberrant behaviour and psychoanalysis and even the anti-psychiatry of such as Thomas Szasz and Wilhelm Reich became intellectually fashionable and culturally influential. In a revaluation of all values, the movies and TV discovered new heroes and new villains. William Lind of the Free Congress Foundation commented:

"The entertainment industry has wholly absorbed the ideology of cultural Marxism and preaches it endlessly not just in sermons but in parables: strong women beating up weak men; children wiser than their parents; corrupt clergymen thwarted by carping drifters; upper class blacks confronting the violence of lower class whites; manly homosexuals who lead normal lives. It is all fable, an inversion of reality, but the entertainment industry made it seem more real than the world that lies just beyond the front door."

Roger Kimball, writing in his own journal *New Criterion* — worthy successor to Eliot's *The Criterion* — says:

"The long march through the institutions signified in the words of Marcuse, 'working against the established institutions while working in them'. By this means — by insinuation and infiltration rather than by confrontation — the counter-cultural dreams of radicals like Marcuse have triumphed."

Traditional Christian culture is now, in Gertude Himmelfarb's words, only "a dissident culture".

This produces in many thoughtful people a spirit of desperation bordering on incredulity – such a man is Cardinal Cormac Murphy-O'Connor, former Cardinal Archbishop of Westminster and leader of the Catholic Church in Britain who asked in his Corbishley Lecture on 28th March 2007, "What kind of culture are we developing which wants increasingly to divorce religion from the public forum?" And he warned, "Religious freedom is not a by-product of democracy but a driving force of it."

The Cardinal explains exactly why the attempt to base democracy on absolute relativism is a contradiction in terms:

"Relativism takes its stand on a desire for equal treatment of different beliefs in the conviction that these beliefs are relative. Yet in contradictory fashion it does so because of a belief in human equality and human dignity which are not relative values. Relativism is no friend of true democracy. By banishing religion from the public realm in the name of equality, it discounts religious perspectives from debate, banishes truth to a private sphere, labels it 'religious' and infers it to be irrational. But in fact truth is not something we construct. It is something we seek together. And there can only be a democratic discussion when truth is a matter of universal concern."

There has been here and there an almost apocalyptic flavour to this chapter and I make no apologies for it, because I believe our situation is dire. But it takes an apparently benign and inconsequential example to reveal just how far our whole culture, civilisation and way of life has been permeated and taken over by the social revolution that is PC. On the face of it, nothing is more benign and respectable than a late afternoon books programme on Radio Four.

One week early in 2007 the guests on this show were discussing their favourite books and they enthused over Evelyn Waugh's novel *Scoop!* Beyond the short discussion about literary style, plot etc, there arose the question, "But, when you were reading it, how did you deal with its political-incorrectness?"

And they all replied, "Oh I just had to ignore it, put it on one side and regard it as a thing of its time".

Those nice people on that books programme really and truly believe that our generation has made moral progress over Waugh's — that views expressed in *Scoop* might have been excused in their day as belonging to a poor, primitive and unprogressed era, but that nowadays, since the coming of the secular gospel of Political-Correctness, we are all so much better and more enlightened. People like so to think of themselves. That is why PC has found such an enthusiastic reception. But it has been the language of the social and cultural revolution which has replaced Christian civilisation.

IV: Is God Intelligent and Did He Design Anything?

Francis Bacon (1561-1626) wrote: "I had rather believe all the fables in the Legend, and the Talmud, and the Alcoran, than that this universal frame is without a mind". Bacon was one of the first experimental scientists and indeed he earned the doubtful distinction of being one of that select band of scientists who killed themselves by their own experiment. For centuries most scientists agreed with Bacon: they did not believe in science as a rival explanation of the world and its origins, but as a method by which the world, created by God, might be better understood.

One of the clearest statements of the belief that God made the world and all that there is comes from William Paley (1743-1805):

"When we come to inspect the watch, we perceive that its several parts are framed and put together for a purpose, e.g. that they are so formed and adjusted as to produce motion, and that motion so regulated as to point out the hour of the day; that if the different parts had been differently shaped from what they are, or placed after any other manner or in any other order than that in which they are placed, either no motion at all would have been carried on in the machine, or none which would have answered the use that is now served by it. . . . the inference we think is inevitable, that the watch must have had a maker — that there must have existed, at some time and at some place or other, an artificer or artificers who formed it for the purpose which we find it actually to answer, who comprehended its construction and designed its use."

This comparison of God to the watchmaker is the most famous exposition of the so called Argument from Design. If the watch requires a designer, says Paley, it is even more obvious that a living creature more complicated than any watch - "in a degree which exceeds all computation" – must have been designed too. Only an intelligent Designer could have created the world and its creatures, just as only an intelligent watchmaker can make a watch:

"The marks of design are too strong to be got over. Design must have had a designer. That designer must have been a person. That person is God."

And, as Paley went on to argue, if God had taken such care in designing even the most humble and insignificant organisms, how much more must God care for humanity!

"The hinges in the wings of an earwig, and the joints of its antennae, are as highly wrought, as if the Creator had nothing else to finish. We see no signs of diminution of care by multiplicity of objects, or of distraction of thought by variety. We have no reason to fear, therefore, our being forgotten, or overlooked, or neglected."

Pierre Simon Laplace (1749-1827) proposed the nebular theory to account for the origin of the solar system and he was asked by Napoleon Bonaparte, "Where does God fit into your system?"

Laplace answered, "Sir, I have no need of that hypothesis"

This reply is often taken to suggest that Laplace was an atheist, but this is not the case. Laplace was only following the scientific method which consists in looking at nature and trying to discover how it works by means of framing hypotheses based on empirical evidence. Laplace was thus saying that God is not part of nature, not part of what might count as empirical evidence. God's existence means something entirely different from what we mean when we say that events exist in nature. So originally in the course of modern science there was no conflict between science and religion which were seen as operating in distinct if complementary spheres of understanding. Certainly science was not thought to *contradict* religion or religion to *nullify* science.

Charles Darwin (1809-1882) did not appear to think that science and religion are at odds. He ended *Origin of Species* with these words:

"Thus, from the war of nature, from famine and death, the most exalted object which we are capable of conceiving, namely, the production of the higher animals, directly follows. There is a grandeur in this view of life, with its several powers, having been originally breathed by the Creator into a few forms or into one; and that, whilst this planet has gone cycling on according to the fixed law of gravity, from so simple a beginning endless forms most beautiful and most wonderful have been, and are being, evolved."

Strict atheists believe that there is no reason to believe in God and that consequently religion is bunk. Here one might ask a preliminary question about the meaning of *no reason*. One might argue, for example, that, since everything we observe seems to have been caused, then the universe itself was probably caused or created too. And if it was created, then there must be a Creator. Again one could suggest that the experience of humankind over millennia has produced a great number of individuals — not otherwise disqualified by stupidity - who did believe in God, and among them many eminent persons in science. Surely this fact is a reason for believing in God?

This is not to say that because every event seems to have had a cause, then that is *proof* that the universe itself had a cause. Nor am I claiming that because many intelligent and scientifically-minded persons have believed in God, that this fact *proves* the existence of God. I am not talking about proof. I am saying only that the evidence from causation, and the other evidence from the experience and writings of intelligent believers, must at least be allowed to count as reasons for believing in God. To say that these arguments cannot be counted as reasons for believing in God comes pretty close to saying that *nothing* could count as a reason for believing in God. And there is nothing reasonable about that argument!

In fact, that sort of thinking is formally exposed as a fallacy in philosophical logic and even given a name. It is known as *ignoratio elenchi* — roughly translated as *missing the point.* That supposed atheistic argument is even given its own form of *ignoratio elenchi*: it is *ignoratio elenchi* by *high redefinition* — to be precise, by high redefinition of the words "no reason". For the reasons given above may not be convincing. They may not even be very good reasons. For the purposes of this part of the discussion, that does not matter. The point is that to say those arguments present us with *no reason* is to talk nonsense. For if they are not allowed to stand as reasons — even if fairly weak reasons — then it is hard to see how anything could be counted as a reason.

Richard Dawkins is a very militant atheist who claims in his book *The God Delusion* that he will believe only those things for which "there is scientific evidence." This must make life very difficult for Professor Dawkins. For consider his proposition: "I will believe only that for which there is scientific evidence". In order to sustain his argument, he must believe that *that* proposition is true. But its truth cannot be discovered by taking into account scientific evidence — for there is no scientific evidence for it.

Classically David Hume (1711-1776) committed the same error. At the end of his *Enquiry Concerning the Human Understanding* he wrote these famous words:

"When we run over our libraries, persuaded of these principles, what havoc must we make? If we take in our hand any volume, of divinity or school metaphysics, for instance, let us ask, 'Does it contain any abstract reasoning concerning quantity or number?' No. 'Does it contain any experimental reasoning concerning matter of fact and existence?' No. Commit it then to the flames: for it can contain nothing but sophistry and illusion."

In that passage, Hume is telling us what sorts of reasons and what sorts of evidence allow us to consider the possibility of *any* proposition. Very well, let us apply Hume's own strictures to Hume's own argument: does *that passage* contain any abstract reasoning concerning quantity or number? No. Does it contain any experimental reasoning concerning matter of fact or existence? No. Then, following Hume's own advice, we can commit to the flames his view also of what makes a meaningful proposition, of what allows us to consider anything as worth considering.

Hume may have been the first to make this particular mistake and Dawkins perhaps the most recent person to do so. But there have been many others in the history of modern philosophy who have made the same error. In the middle of the 20th century there arose a way of doing philosophy which became dominant for fifty years. It was called Logical Positivism. Its founders and chief exponents were Germans and Austrians who formed the Vienna Circle — Schlick, Carnap and others — and its famous populariser in Britain was A.J.Ayer (1910-1989) whose book *Language, Truth and Logic* (1936) was a bestseller.

The Logical Positivists coined a maxim which defined their method in philosophy — which in fact said what forms of philosophical reasoning are cogent and valid and which are not. Their maxim was much like that of Hume, much like that of Dawkins: "The meaning of a statement is its method of verification". Apart from the fact that there is a certain obscurity involved in the idea that a *meaning* might be a *method*, the maxim is flawed, for the same reason that Hume's and Dawkins' definitions are flawed. One has only to ask, "If the meaning of a statement is its method of verification, how does one set about verifying *that?*"

It is not mathematical and it is not experiential — the only categories for meaningfulness which the Logical Positivists would allow. So, by its own self-definition, Logical Positivism is meaningless.

I hope I have not given the impression that all modern scientists are militant atheists. There are agitprop groups of scientists and philosophers here and there who make a career out of being antipathetic towards religion. But many, even most, scientists either have a personal religious belief or at the least they are willing to admit that religious belief is a reasonable option. John Polkinghorne is an Anglican priest and a scientist, one of only two priests who are also Fellows of the Royal Society. Polkinghorne is one of many scientists working today who have written sympathetically about the relationship between science and religion. Polkinghorne does not commit himself to the narrow, and ultimately self-defeating, presuppositions of such as Richard Dawkins and he certainly does not go in for Dawkins' silly *ad hominem* diatribes against religious believers.

He comments on Dawkins' book as follows:
"I have read *The God Delusion* and it is just an atheistic rant - a very disappointing book. Much of it is taken up with stories about religious people

who have done terrible things or said foolish things. Of course, this has happened. But there is no honest recognition in the book of the many occasions on which religious people have done good deeds, of compassion, peacemaking and artistic creativity, or said wise and insightful things. Nor is there adequate recognition that many non-religious people have also done terrible things or said foolish things."

Ian Robinson, who is not a scientist but one of the most penetrating literary critics of our time, author of the influential *The Survival of English*, has, in his article *The Incompetent Atheist*, conclusively repudiated Dawkins' arguments as specimens of incoherence. Robinson quotes from *The God Delusion* the nub of Dawkins' argument for atheism:

"Either God exists or he doesn't. It is a scientific question...the existence of God is a scientific question like any other."

But if the existence of God is a question to be answered by applying the scientific method, this presumes that God is *an object of science* along with all the other phenomena which science explores throughout the universe. As Robinson says,

"Dawkins naturally uses the Bertrand Russell example of the celestial teapot. If someone asserts that there is a teapot in orbit round the earth, but unfortunately too small to be detected by any scientific means, he cannot be proved wrong but the chances of his being right are negligible."

In fact, Dawkins uses Russell's example precisely:

"Russell's teapot of course stands for an infinite number of things whose existence is conceivable and cannot be disproved."

Therefore, we are invited — though brow-beaten into would be a better description of Dawkins' method - to conclude that God is like the teapot — just one more thing among all the other things in the universe. This is a quite astonishingly ignorant conjecture on Dawkins' part and it demonstrates, among other things, that he knows no theology. For no biblical writer, whether Jew of the Old Testament or Christian of the New, no Father of the Church, no Schoolman, no religious philosopher ancient or modern, has ever to my recollection claimed that God is but one object among all the objects in the universe. What the Bible, Jewish and Christian theologians do say emphatically is that the Being of God is a different sort of being from the being of the universe. All these theologians have a technical usage in which they describe this difference: the universe is made up of *creatures* of whom God is the *Creator*.

Let us provide an analogy. Suppose I show you a spanner and ask you to admire the workmanship of the engineer who made the spanner. Wouldn't I suggest that someone take you off to the funny farm if you were then to say: "There is no engineer — because I cannot detect anywhere an engineer who is a spanner". But this is Dawkins' position exactly.. For just as the engineer and the spanner are different in the types of things that they are, so God and the universe are different sorts of beings. I remember a word from the great theologian John Macquarrie which is very much to the point here:

"God does not exist as the world exists. God is the one who allows everything that exists to exist."

In short, God is the Creator.

Incidentally, if Dawkins really does maintain that every intelligible question is a scientific question, then he is making a lot of trouble for himself. For science is based on observation and science itself has concluded that we are able to observe (by any means) only about 4% of the total amount of matter in the universe. The rest cannot be observed and has therefore been described as "dark matter". So 96% of the universe is, so far as we — including scientists - are concerned is effectively *missing*. Now the question arises: in any scientific experiment — even one set up by Richard Dawkins — would a 4% sample be regarded as statistically significant enough to allow any conclusions to be drawn about the nature of the whole? Of course not.

Robinson underlines his refutation of Dawkins' ignorance and silliness:

"Dawkins supposes that 'I believe in God' - as the Nicene Creed begins — really means 'I believe that in the physical universe there is an object called

God.' But no creed in Christendom has ever declared anything so stupid. No orthodox Christian (theologian or not) has ever supposed God to be an object of the same kind (though bigger than?) a teapot."

Crucially, Robinson turns Dawkins' argument back on its perpetrator and says that if God really is as Dawkins describes him, then he is not God and atheism is proved:

"If the God who created the heavens and the earth, and man in his own image, is one object among others, then God as asserted in the creeds certainly does not exist... A man, whether it be John Stuart Mill or Bertrand Russell or Richard Dawkins who does not know that the existence of God is not a scientific hypothesis, can have nothing to say about religion."

Dawkins ought to have done his homework:

"It may be that those who believe in God are making no sense and that their activities are, as Dawkins supposes, all nonsense. But before reaching that conclusion, you have to find your way about the subject. When he discusses religion, Dawkins does not know what he is talking about. And to loose off boisterous opinions about something one does not understand is the first mark of the *uneducated*."

In *The God Delusion* Dawkins has vividly shown himself up as a fool. The fact that this has not been generally pointed out in the reviewing media is an indication of just how far intellectual standards, the ordinary rules of reasoning, have fallen in the numbskull media environment. If a first year student in my philosophy class had produced the argument Dawkins has produced, I would tell him to give up brainwork and do something physical and useful, like cutting the grass.

Perhaps answers to prayers would be evidence that there is a God? Dawkins considers this and so, as man of science, purposes to set up an experiment which he calls "The Great Prayer Experiment." He was serious about this, for he reports that $2.4million was spent on it. Robinson describes the procedure and comments on it.

"This, Dawkins reports, was carried out by strict scientific standards, with a control group for whom no prayers were made. Those who prayed 'were given only the first name and the initial letter of the surname of the patient for whom they were to pray.'

"In the interests of standardisation, they were all told to include in their prayers the phrase, 'for a successful surgery with a quick, healthy recovery and no complications.'

"But this was not prayer. Even if the people praying sincerely believed they were praying (and what test is there of that?) "Thou shalt not tempt the Lord thy God."

"But this was explicitly an attempt to carry out an experiment on God. Presumably the prayers included no such clause as is always implicit and often explicit in Christian intercessory prayer, 'If it be thy will'

Dawkins doesn't understand what prayer is. Any grown up believer could have told him, if he had not been too arrogant to ask. Prayer for, say, a sick person is to bring that person before God, to ask for his recovery, but to rest confident in whatever the will of God is. Christ in the Garden of Gethsemane, asking to be spared crucifixion, is the model for all prayer:

"Father, if thou be willing, remove this cup from me: nevertheless, not my will but thine be done."

Dawkins cannot understand even the elementary aspects of religious belief, but this does not deter him from rushing to try to refute one of the greatest Christian theologians, St Anselm (1033-1109). Dawkins says,

"It is possible to conceive, Anselm said, of a being than which nothing greater can be conceived."

Robinson comments: "On the contrary, Anselm not only never says that God is conceivable, he explicitly denies it — *Es quiddam majus, quam cogitari posit.*"

The way Dawkins approaches theology is as if I should propose a new theory in genetics by consulting the Tarot cards.

Nevertheless, Dawkins has a point — that it is not actually the point he makes is by and by. But if God exists, then there ought to be some evidence of his existence and the only question remaining is of what kind this evidence is. Believers would cite answers to prayers as evidence — that they are assured in the hearts of the presence of God; that God truly influences their lives and morality and so on. Or one might offer the Bible as the revelation of God's existence and the history of his operations in the world. But these are evidences which concern the believer. Is there any evidence for God's existence to convince the open-minded enquirer after truth?

The heavens, the works of thy fingers: the moon and the stars which thou hast made

It used to be believed that the world is ultimately constructed out of tiny particles called atoms. Then it was discovered that these atoms contain even smaller bits: protons, electrons and neutrons. After this were discovered the even smaller sub-atomic particles — the quarks and the neutrinos and even one called "charm." Moreover, it was demonstrated, the interior of the atom is not a miniature solar system with the sub-atomic particles orbiting the nucleus in an orderly, planet like, fashion; but the goings-on inside the atom are so unpredictable that they can only be assessed statistically.

And then it was found that even to observe the movements of the particles is to change their movement. And that in fact the particles seem sometimes not to be particles at all, but more like waves. Then along comes quantum mechanics to inform us that a particle may be (or appear to be) in more than one place at one time; and that it might "move" from one place to another without travelling the distance between the two points.

The physicist Gerald R. Schroeder in his *The Hidden Face of God* summarises this state of affairs:

"The world we see as solid is made solid not by matter but by ethereal forces carried in photons (themselves a theoretical construct) travelling immense distances between the nuclei and surrounding electron clouds.

"The world of atoms and molecules consists of wavelike particles separated from each other by voids, held in place by never seen massless photons travelling at the speed of light among particles that are not only particles but also waves. If you can conceptualise this melee in an intelligible way, I have an urgent suggestion: publish."

Of course, not even the most marvellous complexity proves the existence of God, but to observe this complexity prompts the question: "Is it more likely that all this came into being by accident, or does it show evidence of having been designed?"

In a vivid sentence, the renowned astrophysicist Professor Fred Hoyle answers this question as follows,

"Life evolving by chance has the same likelihood as a tornado blowing through a scrap yard and leaving behind it a fully-formed jumbo jet".

Modern physics reveals to us a world which does not look at all as if it's made of bits and pieces of matter, but is really rather ethereal. Less as if it's material stuff. More as if it's mind stuff. Moreover, it looks overwhelmingly as if the universe was made with us in mind, for, if it had been ever so minutely different, we wouldn't be here. The odds against the universe happening by accident to be so accommodating to us are so astronomical as to be virtually impossible. And, note, it is not theologians who are making this point, but scientists.

There appear to be physical rules in operation throughout the universe governing four principal forces acting reciprocally. These are the strong nuclear force, the weak nuclear force, the electromagnetic force and the force of gravity. If these had been even minutely different both individually and in their relation to one another, the universe would never have been.

Schroeder comments:

"From the 10-to-the-minus-five metres of an organic cell to the 10-to-the-twenty-six metres of the universe, from the mass of an atom, 10-to-the-minus-twenty-six kilograms, to the mass of the sun 10-to-the-thirty kilograms, it's one set of laws. Why?"

As Freeman Dyson said, "Nature has been kinder to us than we had any right to expect."

They have even coined a phrase to refer to the hospitableness of the universe: they call it *The Anthropic Principle* — because the world seems to have been constructed with man in mind. Dawkins and his school might reflect on the fact that we are able to understand at least a little of the universe only because the universe is intelligible. It is the innate intelligibility of the universe which makes science possible. That intelligibility was not created by man or imposed on the universe — at least that much must be conceded if science itself is to be regarded as a way of discovering truth, and not merely a game.

What we perceive in the ordered structure of the vast materials of the universe we see also in the lives of minute living cells. Every cell in the human body forms two thousand proteins every second. Every cell repeatedly selects half a million amino acids made up of ten million atoms. This is not arbitrary. Each protein is designed individually for a specific purpose.

Schroeder offers a picturesque analogy of each living cell:

"Picture a three-dimensional intersection of several major, multi-lane highways, crossovers, on and off ramps, an interlacing of clover-leafs one above the other, traffic moving in all directions. Now take it down, with no loss of the complex weave, to a millionth of a metre and repeat it ten thousand times in a sphere thirty millionths of a metres in diameter — and you've got an inkling of a single biological cell."

The idea that all the manifest orderliness of the cosmos and of the human organism came into being by chance is so absurd as to be beyond belief. Hoyle's image of the Jumbo jet returns to mind. Or imagine, if you can, the

106

game of chess coming into being by chance. If anyone did in fact try to maintain such patent absurdities, we would take him on one side and point out quietly that he did not understand the concept of *chance*. That is not how chance works. And faced with such overwhelming evidence of design, the onus of proof is not on those who believe in a designer, but on those who against all the odds persist in denial.

But there is an even more powerful argument in favour of the belief that the world was designed. *We* human beings understand the concept of design and indeed we go on to design things ourselves. Is it really plausible to suggest that the concept of design arose out of chaos and randomness? Why ever should it do that? The Bible does not go in for explicit philosophical arguments of the academic sort, preferring instead the use of poetry — a word which means *making* — and allusion. So the Bible begins by saying that God made the world and then he made man "in his own image". This means that the God who created order also created humankind capable of understanding this order.

Part of the understanding of the orderliness of the world — trying to discover how it works — constitutes the history of science. But it would be a mistake to assume that science is an sequential progress of knowledge, one scientific truth added to another, until there is the whole body of scientific knowledge. This is a common view of science, but it is entirely wrong. Science does not proceed by adding to previous knowledge but by taking away. The phlogiston theory of the role of the atmosphere in incandescence was supplanted by the discovery of oxygen. The physics of Isaac Newton is not a body of cast-iron laws but a theory superseded by Einstein's discoveries. The atomic theory which said that atoms are the smallest possible particles has been shown to be wrong. It has been said that the whole history of science is repudiation of itself: and that each beautiful hypothesis is in turn destroyed by the discovery of one brute new fact.

The heavens declare the glory of God, and the firmament sheweth his handy-work (Psalm 19:1)

107

V: The History of God and His Enemies
The Bible

There is no atheism in the Bible. This does not mean that everyone believed in God. But the detached and abstracted way of thinking favoured by modern academics was not something shared by the people of either the Old Testament or the New. I don't mean to suggest that everybody in the Bible was faithful and God-fearing. Far from it. The Old Testament prophets are full of denunciations of the disobedient and all those who turn away from God:

"Ah sinful nation, a people laden with iniquity; a seed of evildoers, children that are corrupters: they have forsaken the Lord..." *Isaiah 1:4*

"Can a maid forget her ornaments, or a bride her attire? Yet my people have forgotten me days without number, saith the Lord..." *Jeremiah 2:32*

"Thou hast borne thy lewdness and thy abominations, saith the Lord. For thus saith the Lord God; I will even deal with thee as thou hast done, which hast despised the oath in breaking the Covenant..." *Ezekiel 16: 58-59*

"Ye have borne the tabernacle of your Moloch and Chiun your images, the star of your god which ye made to yourselves. Therefore I will cause you to go into captivity..." *Amos 5:26*

There is no technical atheism in the Bible then, but there is a great deal of turning away from God. The people are chastised for forgetting God, or for putting something else before the commandments of God. The ancient Israelites treasured their close, special relationship with God — the conviction that they were chosen by God. But, being human, they frequently denied this relationship by their disobedience and for this they were excoriated by the prophets, and sometimes in the most tender and heartbreaking words. Hosea, for instance, has God weeping for Israel, his "unfaithful wife."

True, Psalm 14 begins, "The fool hath said in his heart there is no God." But even this is not intellectual atheism. Rather the Psalmist is lamenting the folly of the people for their forgetting God. The great Hebrew scholar Artur Weiser in his commentary on *The Psalms* remarks:

"It is characteristic of the biblical idea of God that this statement is not meant to be understood as a reflection on the existence of God and thus not as some kind of dogmatic atheism, but as a *practical atheism* which tries to elude the demands which the reality of God makes on man's life."

The message is the same in the New Testament: people are not called to air their christological theories but to put their trust in the person of Christ:

"For God so loved the world that he gave his only begotten Son, that whosoever believeth in him should not perish but have everlasting life" — *St John 3:16*

The emphasis is not abstracted and theoretical. Instead the language of the Bible exhorts people to a close relationship with God as a person and this language is full of figures of speech borrowed from daily life. We are urged to *hear his voice* and to *walk in his ways*, to *take my yoke upon you*.

The issue in biblical times and in the early church was not that of God's existence, but of what kind of God is the true God. To put this in the sort of language used by the Bible, it is a question of God or false gods — idolatry. Even the philosophically-minded Athenians were inclined to doubt one god only in the name of another. As St Paul, reported in *The Acts of the Apostles*, says,

"For as I passed by and beheld your devotions, I found an altar with this inscription: TO THE UNKNOWN GOD. Whom therefore ye ignorantly worship, him I declare unto you." — *Acts 17:23*

Atheism in the theoretical, propositional, sense is a modern phenomenon. Even among the scholastic philosophers of the Middle Ages, there was little in the way of an abstracted sense of belief in God. St Thomas Aquinas famously supplied five so-called proofs of the existence of God – except he did not call these *proofs* but *ways*. The Five Ways were a means of demonstrating what was already believed, even what was already taken for granted as given. In short, in the Medieval world view, metaphysics preceded epistemology and the existence of God was an example of what R.G. Collingwood has called "an absolute presupposition." Actually, St Thomas says at the start of Summa Theologiae, "I do in fact hold that the proposition God exists is self-evident in itself."

The Reformation and the Enlightenment

Intellectual atheism, that is the explicit propositional denial of God's existence is an essentially modern phenomenon.

The Enlightenment began with a huge shift in perspective. Medieval philosophical theology began with the being of God and deduced or inferred its conclusions from there. That is, philosophical theology, anthropology, sociology and all the sciences were rooted in metaphysics. Beginning with Descartes, this metaphysical foundation was set aside and the basis of human knowledge began with speculative reasoning. Pope John Paul II commented on this shift in perspective:

"After Descartes, philosophy became a science of pure thought. Both the created world and the Creator remained within the ambit of Descartes' 'I think, therefore I am' as the content of consciousness. God was reduced to an element within human consciousness and so God was no longer considered to be the ultimate explanation for human beings".

In saying these things, John Paul put himself in the company of two of the most original minds of the 20th century: Ludwig Wittgenstein and C.H.Sisson. In his *Philosophical Investigations*, Wittgenstein exposes Descartes' "I think, therefore I am" as a piece of philosophical nonsense. He does this chiefly by means of what has become known as the private language argument. For Descartes even to begin to be able to say "*I* think, therefore *I* am" he would need a language. And language is by definition public. Therefore "I think, therefore I am" is an impossible place from which to start a programme of philosophical speculation. Besides, there is a certain absurdity in my thinking that my own existence is more certain than God's existence; and that therefore I must prove my own existence as a necessary prelude to proving the existence of God.

And what is the actual content of "I think, therefore I am". What is this *I* which Descartes claimed to have identified? Clearly, it is not his body. The first "I" in "I think, therefore I am" cannot be the personality either; for nowhere has Descartes established anything so coherent as the human personality. There is no demonstration of the alleged fact that the *I* is the originator of the *think*. Descartes would have been more accurate if he had confined himself to saying, "There are thoughts". But *whose* thoughts? To claim that they belong to me — to the *I* — cannot be justified in logic. And the *cogito* turns out to be a tautology.

C.H. Sisson said, "The 'therefore' of Descartes now looks like a confidence trick". And so it is. It is a tautology which seeks to prove its point by a piece of mere repetition: the "I" whose existence Descartes is seeking to prove is simply assumed by the "I" who asserts it. Wittgenstein again: "It is as if a man should buy several copies of the same newspaper to find out if what it says is true".

Before Descartes, Shakespeare had worried about this shift in perspective from the theocentric to the anthropocentric. Shakespeare clearly brooded about this shift in metaphysical and theological perspective, and as a supreme, intuitive dramatist he saw this in its psychological aspect. There was a shift from *being* to *thinking about being* or *being as it is thought*. Shakespeare knew this and it worried him so much that it haunts the whole of *Hamlet*:

To be or not to be, that is the question
Sicklied o'er with the pale cast of thought
There is nothing either good or bad but thinking makes it so.

There is even a cross-reference to Luther in Hamlet's dilemma

What think you of Wurtemberg?

In these ways the 16th century marked the deposition of God and the exaltation of man. Man defined himself as the centre of the world and of all apprehension. God was still believed in, but the belief became prior and antecedent to the God believed in. Martin Luther (1483-1546) believed in God passionately and had a troubled emotional relationship with him all his life. But for Luther his powerful emotional apprehension of God was antecedent to the being of God himself. The world of the Reformation was the precise inversion of the Medieval age and it corresponded to the revolution in cosmology also taking place at the time. Man-centred consciousness replaced God-centred consciousness just as Copernicus had replaced Ptolemy.

In the Protestant churches the Real Presence of God in the Blessed Sacrament was denied and replaced by something filtered through the mind. Cranmer in his Consecration Prayer in the 1552 Prayer Book goes out of his way to deny the Real Presence of God in the sense of Transubstantiation — for the whole philosophy of substance, of being, is precisely what is being rejected. And the Sacraments become *signs* — that is not fundamental realities, but realities in their relationship with thought and interpretation. But Cranmer too forgot the commandment which prohibits images. He will not allow relics and images of the saints. But he has an image in the form of a linguistic sign in place of the reality of the Blessed Sacrament.

This development was only the beginning of a long story. The Reformers said, as it were,

"You need God, but you don't need this affirmation of God's substantial presence guaranteed by the words of the priest. You don't in fact need the priest or the Catholic Church. You can retire to your own bedchamber and communicate with God. And that is the only possible sort of communication with God. Of course, you can still reason about God as the scholastics did."

A century later at the Enlightenment the story had developed and became something like this:

"Not only do you not need priests and the church, you don't need God. All you need is Reason."

Atheism as the pretext for anti-religion began at the Enlightenment. Voltaire (1694-1778) said, "Religion must be destroyed among respectable people and left to the mob for whom it was made".

And of course such as Rousseau and Voltaire, philosophers of the Enlightenment, renounced God and said we should rid ourselves of the Christian religion altogether. Voltaire's saying about religious belief being only for the riff raff gives early warning of Marx's remark about its being the opium of the masses. The *Philosophes*, the Encyclopaedists, Diderot, would hear nothing of revelation through the Scriptures. All must be based on the unaided reason. But what if that reason itself is based on something as suspect as "I think, therefore I am".

The rejection of God and the philosophy of being — the replacement of metaphysics by epistemology — is not the whole story of the shift from theocentricism to anthropocentricism. There is also involved the denial of traditional Christian psychological understanding: the doctrine of man. Tradition, even as far as the Reformation — and many devout Protestants would like to say *especially* the Reformation — understood humankind as fundamentally disordered, and this view was expressed in the doctrine of Original Sin. We tend to go wrong. There is nothing odd or occult about this. It is not a quasi-metaphysical taint. It is just the practical problem described by St Paul in words of one syllable:

"The thing I would not, that I do; and what I would, I do not."

Surely that may be held to be the common experience of humankind? Former Bishop of Durham David Jenkins refers with good northern bluntness to

114

Original Sin as "the buggeration factor."

Original Sin was precisely what Rousseau denied. Rousseau preached the doctrine of the Noble Savage — we were all just fine until civilisation and laws interrupted our prehistoric paradisal sojourn. And if we are not fundamentally flawed and imperfect, liable to go wrong, in need of God's forgiveness and reparative Grace, then we are perhaps perfectible. And so the modern doctrine of *progress* was born. Nowadays moral progress of both the individual and his civilisation is assumed. Politicians and the mass media always use the word *medieval* to mean dark, cruel and primitive. But, as noted in the earlier review of the New Morality of the 1960s, beside the horrors of the 20th century — the first century actually to believe the doctrine of progress — the middle ages were comparatively civilised, peaceful and pleasant.

The invention of "progress" in the 19th century

Every age writes its own epitaph. A good summary of the 19th century's self-reflection is Matthew Arnold's (1822-1888) poem *Dover Beach*:

"The sea is calm tonight.
The tide is full, the moon lies fair
Upon the straits..."

It is a beautifully effective evocation of the English Channel by moonlight and it is at once Romantic and Modern. There are no archaisms of the sort that litter second-rate Romantic verse of the period. It does not self-consciously, still less self-indulgently, draw attention to itself. It is full of *things*:

"Of pebbles which the waves draw back and fling
At their return up the high strand..."

There is no striving for effect. The words are allowed to do their own evoking. But the second part of the poem — for which it is chiefly remembered — is less successful for it makes the analogy, implicit in the first stanza, too explicit and so instead of *evoking*, it merely *explains*.

"The Sea of Faith
Was once too at the full..."

You feel like saying, "Ah, so you're telling us that, just as the tide goes out, religious faith recedes as well. How interesting!" But analogies and metaphors should not explain themselves for, if they have to explain themselves, it just means they are unsuccessful figures of speech. Whereas, as Ezra Pound (1885-1972) said:

"The object is the adequate image. Don't keep saying things like, 'dim lands of peace"

The most important aspect of Arnold's poem is that it is so representative of 19th century consciousness. In that age, religion was reduced to psychology and religious attention declined into *feeling*. The subject is not God or religious faith, but how exquisitely the poet feels about his faith – or in this case the loss of faith. No argument is expounded as to why faith has sounded out,

"Its melancholy, long, withdrawing roar"

And this refusal to engage in argument is the signature of that most talkative era. Millions of words were exchanged in religious controversy: the long spat between Newman and Kingsley which at least produced the classic *Apologia Pro Vita Sua* and the even longer controversy about ritual and liturgy; the big row occasioned by discoveries in geology and the bigger row arising out of *The Origin of Species*. But for all the disagreement, there is little in the way of engaged argument: rather we observe the spectacle of men shouting at one another from entrenched – but never properly elucidated – ideological positions. Shelley's (1792-1822) atheism is no argument against religious belief: the poet merely enjoys a long shout against God whom he hates.

The spirit of the 19th century was a burgeoning liberalism, utilitarian, materialistic and shallow. Its most renowned exponent, John Stuart Mill (1806-1873) declared in *Utilitarianism* that happiness should be the overriding aim in the life of every individual:

"The creed which accepts as the foundation of morals Utility, or the Greatest Happiness Principle, holds that actions are right as they tend to promote happiness, wrong as they tend to promote the reverse of happiness."

True, Mill has a little more moral scruple than Jeremy Bentham (1748-1832) who, when it came to the evaluation of happiness, said, "Pushpin is as good as poetry," — a pre-echo of our own "Whatever turns you on" - but he never even comes near a reasonable exposition of the Principle of Utility. How do we assess the value of the intense pleasure of a small group of people at the expense of the considerable distress of a larger group? Am I justified by the Principle of Utility in playing my recording of Beethoven's *Fifth* loudly in the late evening to the irritation of my neighbours? In vain we ask Mill, "How loud? How late in the evening? For how long? How many neighbours?" Bentham's Pleasure Principle and his Utilitarian Calculus were despised by Nietzsche as "pig philosophy" — but Mill is little improvement on Bentham.

There are huge holes in Mill's arguments. He claims: "We can never be certain that the opinion we are endeavouring to stifle is a false opinion; and if we were sure, stifling it would be an evil still."

I suppose English gentlemen talking agreeably over the port after a good dinner would agree with him and relax completely in their quibbles about whether the grouse had been better than the pheasant. But what about the real world? How about the opinions of genocidal Nazism? Can we *never* be sure that this is wrong? And if we could be sure, would we really be wrong to want to silence it? Mill's Principle of Utility does not — cannot — enable us to decide on serious moral issues such as for instance whether the government has the right to compel the MMR vaccine or allow abortion up to twenty-four weeks.

Mill himself seems to think we should not worry about this, for the Principle of Liberty itself — since it belongs to the category of *opinion* — cannot itself be proved as valid beyond a reasonable doubt. So if someone disagrees and devotes his whole life to the extirpation of every instance of liberty, rational men and Utilitarians must not try to stifle his views. In arguing for liberty, Mill famously included liberty in religion. But his personal view was that religion was fading away and he could hear clearly enough its long, withdrawing roar.

Besides, there is an inherent contradiction in Mill's argument. He says loftily of *all* opinions that we can *never* be sure that any one of them is ever right — except perhaps for the certain proposition that we can never be certain of any proposition! He refutes himself.

One man who did understand the contradictions of liberalism was John Henry Newman (1801-1890) — and long before his reception into the Church of Rome:

"The tendency of the age is towards liberalism. But truly religion must be based on authority of some kind - not upon sentimentality. It is the church which is the only legitimate guarantor of religious truth. The liberals know this and are in every possible manner trying to break it up."

In the middle of the 19th century, Newman understood to what extent the church had imbibed the doctrines of Mill and liberalism in general:

"The Church's highest praise is only that it admits a variety of opinions...But why should God speak unless he meant to say something? If there has been a revelation, then there must be some essential doctrine proposed by it. To suppose that all beliefs are equally true in the eyes of God, provided they are all sincerely held, is simply unreal and a mere dream of reason. A system of doctrine has arisen in which faith or spiritual-mindedness is contemplated and rested on as the end of religion and not Christ. And in this way religion is made to consist in contemplating ourselves instead of Christ. Faith and spiritual-mindedness are dwelt on as ends and obstruct the view of Christ. Poor miserable captives to whom such doctrine is preached as the Gospel!

118

What, is this the liberty wherewith Christ has made us free, and wherein we stand, the home of our own thoughts, the prison of our own sensations, the province of self? This is nothing but a specious idolatry."

Newman saw the rot setting in a century and a half ago:

"The spirit at work against Christianity is latitudinarianism, indifference, republicanism and schism - a spirit which tries to overthrow doctrine as if it were the fruit of bigotry, and discipline as if the instrument of priest-craft. The prevailing lies of the age are that there is no positive truth in religion, and that any creed is as good as any other. The lie teaches that all religious declarations are equally worthy because they are no more than matters of personal opinion. The lie teaches that religion is not a truth but a sentiment or a taste; and it is the right of any individual to make of it whatever strikes his fancy."

He expresses in an exact paragraph what he calls "the Principle of Liberalism":

"That truth and falsehood in religion are but matters of opinion; that one doctrine is as good as another; that the Governor of the world does not intend that we should gain the truth; that there is no truth; that we are not more acceptable to God by believing this man than by believing that one; that no one is answerable for his opinions; that they are a matter of necessity or accident; that it is enough if we sincerely hold what we profess; that our merit lies in seeking, not in possessing; that it is a duty to follow what seems to us true; that it may be a gain to succeed, but can be no harm to fail; that we may take up and lay down opinions at pleasure; that belief belongs to the mere intellect, not to the heart also; that we may safely trust to ourselves in matters of Faith and need no other guide."

The Post-Enlightenment liberals who were the establishment in Newman's age believed that reason is immaculate: our feelings may turn us to the bad, but reason is an infallible guide if only we learn to follow its dictates accurately. But Newman reminds us:

"Reason is God's gift; but so are the passions: reason is as guilty as passion."

Moreover, reason does not operate in a vacuum. It is a process which follows from axioms and assumptions. People forget that axioms and assumptions are often little better than prejudices. Reason has to start from somewhere. And in this matter one is reminded of the Irishman who was asked by a tourist how best to get to Dublin; and he replied, "I wouldn't start from here!"

Moreover, Newman says:

"In a state of society such as ours in which authority, prescription, tradition, habit, moral instinct and the divine influence go for nothing, in which patience of thought and depth and consistency of view are scorned as subtle and scholastic, in which free discussion and fallible judgement are prized as the birthright of each individual...all this I own it gentlemen frightens me."

Knowledge, even opinion, has to be based on *something*:

"A question was put to me by a philosopher of the day: 'Why cannot you go your way and let us go ours?' I answer in the name of theology, 'When Newton can dispense with the metaphysician, then you may dispense with us

"Does theology cast no light upon history? Has it no influence on the principles of ethics? Is it without any sort of bearing on physics, metaphysics and political science? Can we drop it out of the circle of knowledge without allowing either that that circle is thereby mutilated or on the other hand that theology is no science?"

In a word, religious truth is not only a portion but a condition of general knowledge. Religious doctrine is knowledge in as full a sense as Newton's doctrine is knowledge. University education without theology is simply un-philosophical. Theology has at least as good a right to claim a place there as astronomy.

He saw through the secularising movement which went under the guise of liberalism while constantly acquiring for itself more centralisation and more authority. He complained:

"It is a growing peculiarity of the present age to purchase a respite from present actual evils by the introduction of it into various departments of the body politic to which it was before a stranger. It is now becoming the fashion to merge the nation with the government, whereas in the past private enterprise had led the way. Waterloo Bridge was built not by the government but by individuals."

Like us, Newman too heard a great deal of chatter about *reforms* in his day and he saw their true purpose:

"Recent reforms are all evidence of the growing popularity of the centralising system. But the destruction of local influences which centralisation involves and the disorganisation of parliament as the seat and instrument of administration tend to increase the power of the executive as the main-spring of all national power and virtually identical with the government.

And he bemoaned the new facts that, "... the magistrate is a paid professional man subject to a distant board and the village constable is superseded by a police officer from a central board and when schoolmasters and schoolbooks are submitted to the government of some foreign authority."

The gradual weakening of religious authority in Newman's time produced a much more powerful secular authority and, worst of all, the merging of the true function of the church with a burgeoning secular bureaucracy He said:

"A whirl of business is always unfavourable to depth and accuracy of religious views."

And, on a subject about which I feel equally rueful as the pile of brown envelopes from the diocesan office gets ever taller,

"There is now too much unavoidable secular business in parish work."

He also saw that secularisation would result in the trivialisation of public life and discourse:

"Every quarter of a year, every month, every day, there must be a supply for the gratification of the public of new and luminous theories. There is a demand for a reckless originality of thought and a sparkling plausibility of argument. They can give no better guarantee for the philosophical truth of their principles than their popularity at the moment and their happy conformity in ethical character to the age which admires them."

The Church of England's response to liberalism and increasing secularisation was — like its response to social change in the 1960s - to compromise and retreat. The church was, in Hulme's phrase, "penetrated by the ideas of its enemies." *Truth* and *dogma* became dirty words. Opinion was all. Only some opinions found more favour than others.

The theories of Marx and Freud, for example, have invaded the theological and pastoral language of modern liberal Christianity and worked a strange and perverse interpretation of faith and morals. Christian counsellors effortlessly articulate the jargon of *repression, projection* and *unconscious motivation.* They have accepted (unconsciously?) Freud's version of psychological determinism and they locate the origin of an adult's psychological and spiritual problems deep in his childhood. Freud, of course, was an atheist, but that does not impede theologians in their enthusiasm for his psychological theories. They may — nominally — reject Freud's atheism while accepting his *insights.* As if his atheism were only accidental, peripheral, to the great truths about human nature allegedly present in his doctrines. But how could the issue of God's existence be merely peripheral? Nobody asked.

Modern theologians are so agile that they see no inconsistency in accepting contradictory determinisms. While they are led by Freud, they also follow Marx. But where Freud declared that sexuality and libido were the principle causes of human behaviour, for Marx the formative influences were all economic. These views cannot *both* be correct. But this does not deter the modern theologians whose motto when it comes to intellectual influences seems to be *A little of what you fancy*. And so they claim that it is economic circumstances which determine behaviour. They are particularly keen to insist that poverty and *underprivilege* are the main causes of crime — an insistence which is both a slur on all that majority of poor people who do not turn to crime and an utter failure in explaining the noted criminal motivations of the rich.

The relativisation of all values is the legacy of 19th century liberalism and progressivism. There was worse to come in the 20th century.

Nothing means anything: Everything means nothing — and nasty with it

At the beginning of the 21st century, we have the philosophical combination of the gospel of meaninglessness with the other gospel of progress. And nobody laughs! For how can there be progress, how can it be measured when anyone's idea of what constitutes progress is as good as anyone else's; and when, in any case words, *texts*, according to Jacques Derrida, don't have meanings? You cannot hold *both* the doctrine of strict meaninglessness — as Heidegger, Sartre, Samuel Beckett and Jacques Derrida do *and* a doctrine of progress — Marx, Comte, Huxley, every modern politician you've ever heard of and the whole mass media.

It is among some of the most prominent literary Modernists themselves that we find the lie given most vividly to the doctrine of progress, to the idea that humankind has improved itself in the present age. There is none nastier than Samuel Beckett.

Here, from *Malone Dies*, is some typical Beckett snide:

"If I had the use of my body, I would throw it out of the window".

123

It is funny but only at the level of disrespect and tastelessness that pissing in an open grave is funny. It is humour in the service of Nothing, and contempt for the human condition. Beckett does not say he would throw *himself* out of the window, for characteristically, there is no self only *it*.

Is the much-vaunted humour really all that sharp? Only if you are creased at the sight of Billie Whitelaw mouthing platitudes and *non sequiturs* while up to her neck in sand. Or if you find hilarious four silent actors moving over and over again from the circumference to the centre of a circle. Or if you're impressionable enough to giggle at an Irishman playing pocket ludo with sixteen sucking stones. He's telling us life is meaningless *again*. It's all he ever tells us. And nihilism does not become true by repetition, only tedious.

Beckett's long literary career and his posthumous acclaim is as the apostle of meaninglessness and fashionable despair. He wrote nothing but discouragement and the intellectuals gleefully cheered every line – but they were only cheering their own vacuity. You might describe his whole oeuvre as *Angst-chic*. The most enthusiastic champions of Beckett are the Hampstead liberals, the metropolitan progressives and chattering classes. Astonishingly, they see no hiatus between their own high-minded social consciousness and the dirt consistently done on humankind by this writer they so idolise.

Beckett's most famous advertisement for nothingness, his play *Waiting for Godot*, was produced near the time of Simone Weil's spiritual masterpiece *Waiting For God*. One detects a deliberate sneer. *Godot* is applauded as an imaginative acceptance of the human condition as meaningless. In it Beckett jibes that Christ was lucky:

"Where he was it was warm and dry and they crucified quick".

Lies. The Gospels tell us Christ hung on the Cross for at least three hours, but what are the Gospels to a bigoted ideological nihilist?

"Nothing is funnier than unhappiness," Beckett chuckles.

The man is a sadist. He spuriously invents his meaningless universe and then casts himself as hero for daring to live in it:

"I can't go on. I'll go on".

It's not courage, only self-indulgence.

He bemoans the writer's predicament:

"The expression that there is nothing to express, nothing with which to express, nothing from which to express, no desire to express..."

It's all baloney. Beckett himself never stops expressing. And he adds,

"...with the obligation to express".

But in a meaningless world, Sam, who or what obliges us?

In Beckett's sordid vision, metaphysics is not the only dead end. Where there is no meaning, there can be no morality. In a nihilistic universe, it is not only the purposes of God and his angels that are meaningless: so also would be our promises, our social contracts, our declarations of loyalty and love.

All worthless. But of course we do love, we do make and even keep promises sometimes; and by these actions we demonstrate that Beckett's world is not merely intellectual incredible, it is ethically perverse as well. And, of course, if the universe is really as meaningless as Beckett says it is, then the claim that Beckett's writing can be described as *true* or even *competent* is merely self-refuting propaganda.

The post-modernity which we now inhabit is a house built on sand, subsiding far from graciously into the morass. We have suffered and brought on ourselves intellectual collapse and the moral and social failure that goes with it. These things are apparent to anyone who will look at a newspaper and television screen or walk down the high street with his eyes open. Western civilisation is dying. As usually happens at the death, people pretend things are really going quite nicely and the prophets of doom are just old misery guts. Bring on the bread and circuses, the plasma TVs and the new generation of mobile phones! Behold the shops are busy and the celebs are celebbing and of course football is always with us. Then one day the economic collapse and the political collapse come together and everybody wrings their hands and cries,

"Why didn't you tell us earlier? We could have done something about it!"

But the answer is always: "Behold they have Abraham and the prophets — let them hear them. Verily they will not believe though one rose from the dead."

Perhaps surprisingly in the light of what has been said here, I should like to end this chapter on a hopeful note. There are possibilities remaining to us even in the heart of darkness. And they arise out of an unexpected quarter — the nihilistic philosophy itself. In his brilliant last book *Memory and Identity*, Pope John Paul II said that all his reading in philosophy had been of St Thomas Aquinas and 20th century phenomenology. At first this seems to be a strange mixture of things to read, but on a closer look it seems this was not such a weird combination after all.

For Heidegger and Sartre, no less than St Thomas, founded their thought on the notion of being. Heidegger's *Being and Time*. Sartre's *Being and Nothingness*. Heidegger speaks of man as *thrown* into the world. Why not say that man was *placed* in the world instead? Heidegger speaks movingly of our *being towards death*. Why not replace this with *being towards life*?

At first I thought these examples might be merely extraordinary — a lucky hit, as it were. But they are not. Gradually it became clear that the thought of Heidegger and Sartre has much in common with that of Aquinas. So much so that if we insert *God* where Heidegger and Sartre say there is nothing, we discover that medieval philosophy and 20th century Existentialism have significant similarities.

Just invert some of the Existentialists' negative sayings - Sartre's

"It is unfortunate for Existentialists that God does not happen to exist."

Let it read,

"It is fortunate that God does exist".

Again Sartre's notorious saying,

"Hell is other people" inverted suggests something very much like

"Love your neighbour as yourself".

Heidegger bemoans the fact of what he calls *inauthentic existence*. Let's be cheerful and speak of *authentic existence* instead. Besides, the Christian faith teaches that there is indeed inauthentic existence: it is the life of sin and the cure is repentance and forgiveness. Sartre has *freedom* as his constant theme. Why should this be the freedom of existential loneliness as he insists? Or the freedom to murder with a machine gun as at the end of Sartre's *Roads To Freedom* trilogy.

"Why not freedom through him whose service is perfect freedom?"

We read the whole of Heidegger's *Being and Time* and the whole of Sartre's *Being and Nothing* and we find the psychological dynamics are the same as those in medieval metaphysics. The only difference is that the one makes God's existence the centre and reference of its whole system, while the other makes God's non-existence the centre and reference. Not a small matter, you might think. But Sartre's and Heidegger's systems lead to *Angst* and despair, and the radical freedom they promise is that of the damned. Aquinas and medieval theology offers deliverance from anxiety — *consider the lilies of the field*, joy and the radical freedom which comes through the worship and service of God. And, to adopt the linguistic strictures of Derrida and the Deconstructionists to the effect that words do not have meanings only functions, then the sort of linguistic inversions I have been suggesting are perfectly valid: make these inversions and see where they lead practically in life as it is being lived.

In summary, Sartre's and Heidegger's thought is metaphysics without fundamental reality. Those two philosophers do not make the mistake of substituting epistemology for metaphysics, as Descartes did and as all western philosophy has continued to do since the Enlightenment. They just start their metaphysics in the *wrong place*: they start with the Cartesian *I*. Man. And this solitary *I* sits calling anxiously into a bleak cold meaningless universe which does not answer back. St Thomas's thought is almost identical — except with him the metaphysical analysis starts with God. And the world which is God's creation is our homeland. This is no sleight of hand. C.H. Sisson said that there is no philosophical difficulty in believing in God:

"All it takes is the removal of the prejudice against God's existence."

People ought to be reassured that it is not foolish for them to put their trust in God. Modern thought has not disproved the existence of God — though it is widely believed to have done so. For modern philosophy itself is based on a mistake. But the being of God is more certain than my being. Let me repeat Sisson's apparently whimsical but actually profound remark:

"The only word in the Creed that gives any difficulty is 'I'"

Precisely. And it turns out after all to be the discredited tautological *I* of Rene Descartes' "I think, therefore I am."

VI: Coming Back to God

Tried and tested traditional patterns of thought and practice were partially restored in Britain during the last thirty years. Economic conservatism transformed the country's finances and improved the personal wealth of the people after the three decades following the Second World War when Britain was hidebound by collectivism, with undemocratic and unrepresentative trades unions holding successive governments to ransom and deciding economic policy. The reforms that have taken place over the last generation, though long overdue, could never by themselves constitute a full restoration of the nation's integrity. Man does not live by market forces alone. As G.K. Chesterton said:

"Since *price* is a crazy and incalculable thing, while *value* is an intrinsic and indestructible thing, they have swept us into a society which is no longer solid but fluid, as unfathomable as a sea and as treacherous as a quicksand.

"Whether anything more solid can be built again upon a social philosophy of values, there is no space to discuss at length here; but I am certain that nothing solid can be built on any other philosophy; certainly not upon the utterly un-philosophical philosophy of blind buying and selling; of bullying people into purchasing what they do not want; of making it badly so that they may break it and imagine they want it again; of keeping rubbish in rapid circulation like a dust-storm in a desert; and pretending that you are teaching men to hope because you do not leave them one intelligent instant in which to despair."

Consumerism and materialism are not enough

It is therefore encouraging to see the revival of the sense of community and belonging and there are signs at last, even in the government, that social problems are not solved merely by throwing money at them. What is required is generous giving but also personal interest and involvement and here in the

City the livery companies set a fine example by their support for community programmes in the East End and beyond. Their contribution is at its best not merely financial but by practical association, working and socialising with the communities they are trying to help.

Insofar as they do this charitable work individuals and institutions go some way towards keeping the biblical commandment to love one's neighbour. There is nothing sentimental about this responsibility as both Old and New Testaments make it plain that each person will be held accountable for how he treats his neighbour. The prophetic tradition in the Jewish faith warns that a people which rejects fair and charitable dealing thereby incurs God's displeasure:

"I hate, I despise your feast days and I will not smell your solemn assemblies....take away from me the noise of thy songs; for I will not listen to the melody of thy viols. But let justice roll down as waters, and righteousness like a mighty stream" — *Amos 5:23-24*

In the New Testament Christ issues terrible warnings to those who neglect their responsibility towards their neighbour:

"Inasmuch as ye did it not to one of the least of these, ye did it not to me. And these shall go away into everlasting punishment" — *St Matthew 25:25-46*

It is also made plain that piety and the strong profession to love God are not enough:

"If a man say, I love God, and hateth his brother, he is a liar: for he that loveth not his brother whom he hath seen, how can he love God whom he hath not seen? And this commandment have we from him, that he who loveth God love his brother also" — *I St John 4: 20-21*

But justice, charity, fair-dealing and social responsibility are not enough. The Judeao-Christian religious tradition makes plain also the requirement to love and serve God. Of the Ten Commandments, the last six spell out our duty towards our neighbour; but these depend on the first four which outline our first duty to God. In the New Testament, Christ delivers our whole responsibility:

"Thou shalt love the Lord thy God with all thy heart and with all thy soul and with all thy strength and with all thy mind; and thy neighbour as thyself" — *St Luke 10:27*

There is no getting away from this dual responsibility. It is not possible to love God while hating our neighbour, but there is no interpreting the commandment to love God as if it were a mere metaphor for loving our neighbour. Over the last generation the church has been very insistent on the love of our neighbour, but coy and shy about proclaiming the prior requirement to love God with our whole heart, soul, strength and mind. But the whole biblical tradition tirelessly repeats and stresses the absolute duty to both parts of the Commandment.

To put this in modern jargon is to say that moral values must be rooted in the apprehension of transcendence. *Pace* Jeremy Bentham, John Stuart Mill and the utilitarian calculus, ethical values are not negotiable: ethics is not some sort of accounting procedure by which we work out the greatest happiness of the greatest number. The Jewish and Christian faiths teach that the origin of morality is a mystery belonging in the being of God himself. T.S. Eliot in *Choruses from the Rock* expresses this memorably:

"However you disguise it, this thing does not change:
The perpetual struggle of Good and Evil.
Forgetful, you neglect your shrines and churches;
The men you are in these times deride
What has been done of good, you find explanations
To satisfy the rational and enlightened mind."

But rationality and enlightenment — those secular terms — are never enough:

"There is no life that is not in community," says Eliot. And how the social-gospellers have agreed with that. But he adds:

"And no community not lived in praise of God."

It is a better way of saying that values without God are no values.

I can speak best about the local community where I live and work — where my church is in the City of London. There is plenty of money here and plenty of tradition. And there are thoughtful, constructive people who have the interests of the community at heart: I have already described the contribution of the livery companies and some of the financial houses to work among the poor. But members of these institutions — with some shining exceptions — are not enthusiastic about God.

There is civic religion. This is like church parade or like a recollection of school chapel. They like to sing the lusty hymns such as *Jerusalem* and *I Vow to Thee My Country*. If they are churchwardens, they like to carry their wands and to march up the aisle two by two, clicking their heels in step, as someone said the other day, not unkindly, "rather like a pantomime horse". They like to come up to the altar and take part in the solemn elevation of the collecting plate. They quite like to be reminded by the preacher that they should be generous with their money and have *a social conscience*. This is civic religion and its adherents are good people, affable enough even to smile when in a sermon, and mixing public school and City metaphors, I caricatured it as "stripey trousers and Spotted Dick."

This is fine as far as it goes, but we are required to go much further. We must recall not only our duty to our neighbour and, as it were sanctify this at the church parade, but our duty to God: the first four Commandments as well as the last six. The Jewish people of the Old Testament were frequently condemned by the prophets for forsaking God and warned that their salvation - their well-being in this life as well as their eternal destiny — depended upon their returning to the worshipping of God and to obeying him. It is the same

132

story again and again. After the Exodus, as soon as the Israelites find the going to be tough in the wilderness, they curse God and cry to be back in the fleshpots of Egypt. God feeds them with manna from heaven. And within days they are grumbling again. Moses ascends Mount Sinai to receive the Ten Commandments and, as soon as his back is turned, the people are dancing before the golden calf. King David is favoured by God. He gains a great empire and establishes Israel among the nations. But he turns from God's Commandments and consequently falls from grace. It is the same story with his son Solomon and with nearly all the Kings of Israel.

And the antidote, the cure for all this woe is also always the same:

"For thus saith the Lord God, the Holy One of Israel; In returning and rest shall ye be saved." — *Isaiah 30:15*

There is no economic programme, no political programme and no social programme that can provide what is required. Any or all of these may be good in themselves, but they are at best only necessary and not sufficient conditions for the right and full conduct of our lives. Religion, despite what some politicians think, is not merely a useful agent of social control — after the fashion of Voltaire who said it is good "for the servants." Religion in the sense of being bound to God, clinging to God, is the inescapable demand.

Jesus repeats the same message in the New Testament:

"The people draweth nigh unto me with their mouth, and honoureth me with their lips; but their heart is far from me. But in vain do they worship me, teaching for doctrines the commandments of men." — *St Matthew 15: 9-10*

Civic religion knows all about honouring with the lips, but its followers do not like to be reminded too strongly of the Commandments of God: they like to think that they have fulfilled the Commandments of God by serving their neighbour. Good as this service is, it is not enough. It is not the centre and purpose of religion. The admonition is to something other, something beyond, in which all human morality is rooted and from which alone we derive our meaning:

"Be not conformed to this world: but be ye transformed by the renewing of you mind, that ye may prove what is that good and acceptable and perfect will of God." — *Romans 12:2*

The tragedy is that many respectable people, influential people here in the City and movers and shakers throughout our great institutions believe that civilisation and a decent going on will just continue without anyone actually having to believe the gospel and say their prayers. In fact it's worse: the modern mindset of some influential and powerful people is that they have actually risen far above Christianity — all those miracles and tall stories about the Resurrection. It was good enough for St Augustine and St Thomas Aquinas, but it's not quite good enough for today's inhabitants of Lombard Street and the very modern and exquisitely refined Master of the Worshipful Company of Screwtop Bottlemakers.

The frivolous state of the English middle class today is seen in its trading on the beliefs and values which it no longer practises. They offer their "support" for Christianity without actually believing it themselves. They come to church only on civic occasions as a ritual form of self-advertisement. If truth be known, they think they have distilled a weak, euphemistic, thoroughly decent - and throroughly useless — imitation of Christianity and they practise something like that satirised in Reinhold Niebuhr's slogan in which:

"A God without wrath brings men without sin into a kingdom without judgement through the ministrations of a Christ without a Cross."

The leaders of our society, politicians, formers of opinion, arbiters of taste and fashion, imagine that our civilisation can continue indefinitely without the absolute truths of religion and morality. And if you believe in absolute values, you're dismissed as a bigot and an obscurantist. Early in 2007, the EU warned Poland that its citizens are too conservative. For Poles were refusing to line up on the "progressive" side on abortion, contraception and euthanasia — preferring the modern gospel of death to the glorious life of the Christian

Church. Modern secular Europe has thus declared war on its own inheritance.

Today's influential people think that our society can prosper without sure faith and absolute morals. They are suspicious of this spiritual stuff: "It's not for me, Rector. I do as I would be done by and I leave the rest to the priests." But it is not enough. Our religion is not priestcraft but the discipleship of all believers. And what does this involve? The answer is unremarkable enough and without novelty or gimmicks. There is no new way of following God, no version of the old faith suitably demythologised and modernised, made appropriate for "man come of age." Religion is not *spirituality* — that sordid cultivation of one's exquisite personality that we find so much of in the bookshops on the *Body, Mind and Spirit* shelf. Religion is not psychotherapy or self-improvement. The practice of religion is nothing but putting oneself in the presence of God and becoming conscious of an utter need of him. It is to realise the plain truth expressed by St Augustine:

"O Lord, thou hast made us for thyself. And our hearts are restless until they rest in thee."

Christian prayer and worship are not a bit of background music while we get on with the social work. Performances in church of such as *The St Matthew Passion* and *The Christmas Oratorio* are not the church's version of secular concerts and still less a *frisson* of cultural excitement to reward highbrow Christians for all they have donated to Christian Aid.

The basic requirements are not complicated: private daily prayer, reading the Bible and receiving the Sacrament of the Holy Communion. Other activities grow out of these fundamentals: studying, learning, speaking to one another about God. Prayer, devotion and worship are not utilitarian acts, things done *so that*. Instead they contain their own purpose within their own logic, and this is simply to draw closer to God and to attempt to fashion one's life according to God's ways. This is as good a definition as there could be of the difference between *sacred* and *secular*. If there is an analogy for the practice of religion, then it is that derived from the artwork: something done for its own sake. Religion does not have a *meaning* if by *meaning* is meant something by which to measure it. Rather, religion is that thing by which all else is measured. It is either that, or it is blasphemous folly.

This is why the world, functional and utilitarian as it is, does not understand religion. It is why many of those who attend church, and even those who say prayers from time to time, misunderstand what it is to be religious. It is why Christ's contemporaries, and even his disciples, did not understand him. They looked at him and wondered what he would *do*, what he would make of himself — as if he might even have a *career*. "What is it to be then, Jesus, freedom-fighter, miracle worker, social worker, exorcist, itinerant healer, crafty preacher or what?" But Jesus said to his disciples:

"If the world hate you, ye know that it hated me before it hated you. If ye were of the world, the world would love his own: but because ye are not of the world, but because I have chosen you out of the world, therefore the world hateth you" — *St John 16:18-19*

The world hates Christ because he is no *earthly* good, and for the same reason Christians misunderstand him still. It is nearly impossible to convince modern people, raised from their earliest schooldays on the utilitarian gospel of *so that*, to understand that there is anything which just *is* or should be done for its own sake. The religious life is a mysterious activity and again the comparison with the artwork is appropriate. The true artist does not know what the painting will finally look like, or what the musical composition will sound like. The true novelist does not know completely what his characters will do. He gives them life and autonomy and they go their own way, sometimes even doing things which the novelist would rather they didn't do. In all these things the artist mimics the creative work of God himself.

If the artist could *explain* his work, there would be no need for his work. The artwork is precisely the way of saying what the artist wishes to say. If he could have said what he wished to say without the artwork, then he would not have put himself to the trouble of producing the work in the first place. There is a story of how Beethoven once played in public his *Appassionata Sonata*. A young woman applauded and said, "That's very fine — but what does it mean?"

Whereupon, Beethoven returned to the piano-stool and played it again.

When I say that the religious life is a mystery, I mean a mystery not like a puzzle-book but in the sacramental sense. The Greek word for a sacrament is μυστηριον - a mystery. And the nature of a sacrament is to embody that which lies beyond the understanding, so that by participating in the sacrament we enter in some degree into what is transcendent. We can no more explain how a sacrament *works* or to what it might lead than we can know the course of a novel before we have read it.

There is another sense in which prayer and the religious life is like the artwork, like the creative activity of God himself; and it is in the trouble it causes us:

"For we know that the whole creation groaneth and travaileth in pain together until now" — *Romans 8:22*

We cannot know the *meaning* of our religious devotion. It is itself the meaning. We are simply commanded to get on with it and, as Eliot said,

"Ours is only the trying: the rest is not our business."

But then I think of all those hardworking, good-hearted City men with their charitable disposition and their civic religion. Their whole lives are conducted *so that*. No wonder they, and the great proportion of humankind, find religion incomprehensible. Tell them it is what we are commanded to do, and they will bridle. They don't like being told what to do: these are the people who tell others what to do. And they are genuinely puzzled by the apparent inconsequentiality of religion. They are like the child at his first cricket match:

"Why is that man hitting the ball with his bat?"

"Because he wants to score runs."

"Why does he want to score runs?"

"So that his side will score more runs than the other side."

"Why does he want his side to score more than the other side?"

"Because then his side will have won."

"Why does he want to win?"

Eventually the patient father becomes exasperated and ends up saying something like: "Well, that's just cricket. That's what cricket *is*."

There are no meta-cricketing questions. And there are no meta-religious questions. Religion is for its own sake.

There is a deeper reason, beyond all the Dawkinsesque pseudo-scientific claptrap, why modern people do not take readily to Christianity: the Christian faith is offensive to modern man's pretensions. It is all encapsulated in one small contrast. Whereas the Bible preaches against self-esteem, the modern world exalts it. But the last thing I should esteem is myself. Self-respect I might strive for — a respect grown out of knowing that I have tried to do as I ought. But self-esteem is nothing but self-regard dressed up in the jargon of psychotherapy. Why do modern types not turn to the faith? Eliot gives a plain answer:

"Why should men love the Church? Why should they love her laws?
She tells them of Life and Death, and of all that they would forget.
She is tender where they would be hard, and hard where they like to be soft.
She tells them of Evil and Sin, and other unpleasant facts.
They constantly try to escape
From the darkness outside and within

By dreaming of systems so perfect that no one will need to be good"
              —   Choruses from the Rock

"Sin" is regarded as an old-fashioned word — something mentioned only by elderly Presbyterian spinsters or tabloid newspapers when they are employing what passes in their imaginings for irony in describing sexual shenanigans. Sin is universally seen as something that is out of date. Why, to call someone a sinner is to offend against his self-esteem. We are progressed and modern people who have no need of such ancient and, worst of all, *unhealthy* words as "sin."

But sin is nothing other than a sense of true perspective, the reality principle. There is much talk of *progress*, but where was the evidence of progress in the trenches and poisoned gas, at Coventry and Dresden, Stalingrad and Hiroshima…at the Rwandan genocide, with napalm, in the light of 200,000 abortions every year in Britain alone and in the whole catalogue of corporate and personal depravity we see all around? And never mind evil on the grand scale, a moment's honest introspection shows that each one of us has regrets over aspects of our past conduct, what Eliot calls,

"Things ill-done and done to others' harm which once we took for exercise of virtue."

We all know that sometimes we fall short. That is what "sin" means. It is a word derived from the archery contests in the Greek games άμαρτια - said of those arrows which fell short. So, when St Paul says,

"For all have sinned and fallen short of the glory of God" — *Romans 3:23*

- it is a black joke.

To speak of sin is not to employ language and concepts which are merely archaic and now useless: it is to understand human psychology. We sin and we fall short. Does anyone seriously deny it — either at the individual or the community level? Of course, sin is not *all* we are. We are capable of goodness, love and self-sacrifice. But sin is where we must start from in any serious attempt to understand the human heart and human nature. The New Testament puts it in words of one syllable:

"If we say we have no sin, we deceive ourselves and the truth is not in us. But if we confess our sins, he is faithful and just to forgive us all our sins and to cleanse us from all unrighteousness" — *I St John 1:8-9*

Is there anything there too difficult for modern man to understand? Why should it strike us as alien and offensive? Isn't the very sensation of our imperfection — intellectual and moral — at the heart of our self-understanding? If it isn't, then we are devoid of understanding — because that is actually how things are with human nature, and we have the history to prove it.

Although our religion begins by asking us to be aware of our own shortcomings, to face reality as it is and not through the tinted spectrum of the narcissistic psychotherapeutic cult which passes for *spirituality* today, our religion does not end there. We are not called to dwell on our sins, for that would be only another version of self-absorption. The Psalmist urges us:

"O be joyful in the Lord" — *Psalm 100:1*

And reminds us of,

"…food out of the earth and wine that maketh glad the heart of man: and oil to make him a cheerful countenance and bread to strengthen man's heart" — *Psalm 104:15*

The New Testament echoes this cheerfulness in Christ's miracle of the water into wine — all 180 gallons of it. (*St John 2:1-11*). And *The Book of Common Prayer* begins every marriage service with a reminder of this joyful miracle.

In his last conversations with his disciples, Christ says:

140

"I am come that ye might have life, and have it more abundantly" — *St John 10:10.*

So the indispensable religion to which we are being called back is not a dark thing, laden with sin and guilt, but full of joy and triumph, in pleasure and, more even than happiness — exaltation. The truth is that whenever people feel moved enough to make a movement back to our religion, they always remark on how enjoyable, cheering and consoling it is. People pour out of Choral Mass at our St Michael's cheered up refreshed and vibrant. But those who have not been to church for years or since they were children in Sunday School, or those who have never been to church in their lives, need a little encouragement. This encouragement sometimes comes in a strange way which is not at all welcome.

The history of God's people's relationship with him is the story of desertion and return, apostasy alternating with renewed devotion: not that God is inconstant, but we are. If that relationship had been an ordinary marriage, it would have ended in divorce ages ago. But God is faithful and he has promised that he will never forsake his people however they abuse his kindness. Indeed, they have already abused his kindness ultimately by putting his Son to death. But God is constant and he will love us though we slay him.

This history of desertion and return is a recurring pattern: it is the *Leitmotif* of human consciousness and conduct and imprinted on the whole career of humanity in our myths, legends and history. In the beginning God gives Adam paradise. Adam disobeys. God's people cry out to him from their captivity in Egypt and God provides Moses to deliver them. As soon as the people fall on hard times in the wilderness, they reject the God who set them free. Time and again through their whole history in the Promised Land, the Kings of Israel and Judah and their people turn away from God. God raises up prophets and calls them to repent and return. This pattern reveals the deep psychological-spiritual flaw in the soul of humankind. It consists in our thinking that we can live our lives independently of God, his ways and his laws. When life is going well with us, we easily believe that we can get by without God. Sooner or later there occurs a catastrophe and in our fear and anguish we ask God to deliver us once again. And so it goes on.

Europe, created out of the classic civilisation and culture of our Jewish-Christian past has had an easy time since the end of the Second World War, and yet again we have seen the loosening of our spiritual ties, our rejection of the faith that has made us. I have spent much ink in these pages describing the character of this rejection in our time. Like the ancient Israelites and many Christian states and communities before us, we have contrived our own style of desertion. But it has been the same old story throughout. G.K.Chesterton in *The Everlasting Man* writes of "the five deaths of the faith

"At least five times, therefore, with the Arian and the Albigensian, with the Humanist sceptic, after Voltaire and after Darwin, the Faith has to all appearances gone to the dogs. In each of these five cases it was the dog that died. How complete was the collapse and how strange the reversal we can only see in detail in the case nearest our own time"

Of course, Chesterton has not lived on into our time and so he could not have seen the particular form of our latest desertion – but he would surely have recognised it as yet one more repetition of the old pattern. In our time secularisation has become the form of our turning away from God. It is the new apostasy, the new atheism, the old disobedience dressed up in all that arrogant chatter about *progress, modernity* and *man come of age*. It amounts to the same thing as all the previous rebellions: simply the assertion by word and deed that we no longer need God. And there is no reason to believe that the pattern will continue in any other way than that which it has taken throughout history and in the myths and legends which were before history. There will be a crisis, a catastrophe so huge and unavoidable, that even modern man with all his *liberated consciousness* will be overwhelmed by it. What form will this catastrophe take?

It will be the same as before, a similar fate to that which overtook Rome: enemies at the gates and decadence within. In our time the unmistakable enemy at the gates is fundamentalist, militant Islam, imperial and aggressive. About the nature of the decadence within, enough has been said in these pages already. The issue is compounded by the fact that the enemy at the gates despises our decadence within. There is going to be a war, a cataclysm and in this war the first shots have been fired already. Here are the words of the President of the Italian Senate:

"Is there a war, perhaps? I answer yes, there is a war, and I believe that the responsible thing to do is to recognise it and to say so, regardless of whether the politically-correct thing to do is to keep our mouths shut.

"In Afghanistan, Kashmir, Chechnya, Dagestan, Ossetia, the Philippines, Saudi Arabia, the Sudan, Bosnia, Kosovo, the Palestinian Territories, Egypt, Morocco and much of the Islamic and Arab world, large groups of fundamentalists, radicals, extremists – the Taliban, Al Qaeda, Hezbollah, Hamas, the Muslim Brothers, Islamic Jihad, the Islamic Armed Group and many more – have declared a holy war *jihad* on the West. This is not my imagination. It is a message they have proclaimed, written, communicated, preached and circulated in black and white. Why should we not take note of it?"

Well, the response to Marcello Pera's question is that, when the bombardments in this war come heavily enough – in New York, in Madrid or in London – we do take note of it. But only for a while. And then, during the ensuing lull, we retire into our drowsy unconcern again. We love our consumerist lifestyle and our secularised permissiveness. We do not want to be reminded about the enemy at the gate and we do not even notice our decadence within.

The President of the Italian Senate describes this mood also:

"A foul wind is blowing through Europe. I am referring to the idea that all we have to do is wait and our troubles will disappear by themselves, so that we can afford to be lenient even with people who threaten us, and that in the end,

143

everything will work our for the best. This same wind blew through Munich in 1938. While the wind might sound like a sigh of relief, it is really a shortness of breath. It could turn out to be the death-rattle of a continent that no longer understands what principles to believe, and consequently mixes everything together in a rhetorical hodgepodge."

By such words, Marcello Pera shows that he is one of the latest is in the long line of prophets raised up by God since the days of man's first disobedience.

I have seen at first hand the threat which he describes and on my own doorstep, in my own house, I have seen the drowsy unconcern of the people, their apathy, their not-wanting-to-know, here in the City of London.

I returned to London from Oxford on the morning after 9/11 and noticed immediately how quiet the streets were in the City. The financial sector was working normally, but people were subdued, silent and introspective. There were no passenger jets flying their usual routes over London. I noticed too that there was a greatly increased attendance at the weekday Masses. People were dubious and hesitant, as if unsure of how they should be responding to what had taken place. There were not ready-made attitudes towards a massive attack on a Western capital. But at the front of everyone's mind was the fear that it might happen again — here in London.

I phoned the Stock Exchange where I was Chaplain and the press offices of a few of the big banks and insurance houses in my parish and told them that I was to put on a Requiem Mass the next day. Two hundred and more people turned up for it — most of them I had never seen in church before. They came in silently. Throughout the proceedings not a single mobile phone went off. I made no concession to the touchy-feely chat show style of worship so characteristic of the decadent Church of England, but said the first part of the service in Latin and the rest from *The Book of Common Prayer*. I thought this would be suitable for Catholics and Protestants alike. I did not preach, but, before the Communion, simply repeated the words:
Requiem aeternam dona nobis Domine: et lux perpetuam, luceat eis.

144

Not a sound. When it was over, they all filed past me in that heavy silence, many of them in tears.

A week later and they were all relieved that there had been no further atrocity. The congregation at the weekday Masses reverted to normal attendance. The streets were all chattering mobile phones again and the wine bars' brisk trade resumed. The threat had gone away. But of course it has not gone away. It persists and it will intensify. Next time, or the time after, it will be bigger, more devastating, perhaps involving nuclear weapons. For this we do not have to await the Iranian bomb: there are enough spare warheads from the collapsed Soviet empire to arm World war III. And there are notoriously unstable nuclear powers, particularly Pakistan, teeming with Muslim militants and with a history of providing training camps and safe-havens for terrorists. That is the scale and scope of the enemy at the gates. What of the decadence within?

Militant Islam looks upon Western society as a wasteland. They despise our cultural decadence, its blatant sexual display and its crass enslavement to the sordid craving for base satisfactions. Devout Muslims urge us to adopt their ethical standards, but we reply, if I may put it hyperbolically: "No thank you. We have standards of our own: sexual licence, drinking and gambling 24/7, celebrity idols and abortion used as a form of contraception. And if you get aggressive with us — we'll fire salvos of condoms at you." To say the least, we are hardly constituted of the moral fibre required to resist the militant Islamic certitude.

The unpalatable truth is that our nation, and beyond it the whole of modernised, secularised Europe, will not do the one thing necessary. We shall not turn again to God until we are overwhelmed and perhaps almost annihilated by some great catastrophe. The most likely form of this catastrophe is an act of terrorism on the grand scale: a nuclear bomb in a suitcase, biological terrorism in our great cities. Nothing in history is *inevitable* — as the Marxists falsely believed - but the coming grand scale terrorist atrocities are as certain as any historical event can be. Our enemies have not forgone such atrocities because they are having mercy on us, but only because they have not managed the practicalities *yet*. Or because their attempts have been thwarted.

There are so many nuclear weapons unaccounted for after the end of the Cold War. In 1991, Dick Cheney, then Secretary of State for Defense, said,

"If the Soviets (*sic*) do an excellent job at retaining control over their stockpile of nuclear weapons — let's assume they've got 25,000 to 30,000, that's a ballpark figure — and they are 99% successful, that would mean you could still have as many as 250 that they were not able to control."

In his book *Nuclear Terrorism*, Graham Allison quotes Tom Ridge, US Secretary of Homeland Security:

"Future attacks will rival or exceed the attacks on New York and the Pentagon. The question is not *if* but *when*."

President Ahmadinejad of Iran is a fundamentalist Shi'ite Muslim who has stated that he believes it his religious duty to promote the last battle — the Bible calls it Armageddon — in order to reveal the Tenth Iman, a mystical Islamic figure who will bring about the end of the world and the final judgement. Ahmadinejad has stated that a prelude to this cataclysm will be the destruction of Israel — a task which he has vowed to complete. Iran, which describes the West as its eternal enemy, the Great Satan, will shortly be in possession of its own nuclear arsenal. But we may not have to wait even a few years. Pakistan already has the nuclear bomb, and Pakistan is a violently unstable fundamentalist Muslim hotbed, only temporarily in alliance with the West. Its President is despised by the Islamists for making this alliance and he could be removed any day.

Whether the huge coming atrocities will be perpetrated by hostile national governments, by covert state sponsored terrorists or by international terrorist groups such as Al Qaeda acting alone, the atrocities will come. Of course Christians do not hope for these atrocities. But the atrocities will come — that much is certain. To pretend that nothing of the sort will happen is only wishful thinking which goes along with the foul wind of appeasement spoken of by Marcello Pera. When the calamity strikes, then Europe including Britain will be shaken to its roots and will turn again to its historic religious tradition for explanation, comfort and relief.

It is not God who will deal out this catastrophe as a form of punishment. We shall bring it on ourselves. God is the one we shall turn to desperately seeking relief. And in this we shall simply be following the old pattern that goes back to biblical times: the Israelites' desertion at the time of the Golden Calf and the repeated disobedience of the kings of Israel and Judah, followed in our own time by the many apostasies perpetrated by Christians.

We have been warned countless times in our Scriptures that catastrophe is what always happens when we forsake God and our religious faith. But we never believe it. We imagine that our own generation is not like those which went before. We think of ourselves as somehow *exceptional*. And the particular character of our exceptionality today is that we think of ourselves as having outgrown all that primitive biblical stuff and that the eternal moral law no longer applies in our case. And we are persuaded of our omnipotence by our technological progress which makes it look as if there is nothing we cannot do. Such a thoroughly modern people as we are today are surely not in the same case as those ignorant primitives! But those ancient people were not primitive. And we are in exactly the same case as they were. Because the cataclysm is delayed, we imagine it will never happen.

But let us listen again to what the prophecies of our sacred Scriptures actually say. Here are some words from *A Commination* from *The Book of Common Prayer* which is set to be read every Ash Wednesday:

"The day of the Lord cometh as a thief in the night: and when men shall say, Peace and all things are safe, then shall sudden destruction come upon them as sorrow cometh upon a woman travailing with child; and they shall not escape."

What is to be done in the interim? What should philosophers, teachers and priests say? The repeated pattern of history — our desertion of God always followed by catastrophe — may be held up ever so boldly before the people, but there will not be many who take heed. People do not heed warnings. They deride the prophets, calling them pessimists, doom-mongers — and worse. People do not heed warnings. They heed catastrophes, belatedly. The background *leitmotif* to our human experience is the clatter of the stable door being shut after the horse has bolted.

If the great mass of the people will not return to God, what should religious people do? There is a widespread sense of dismay and depression among Christians. We see the faith threatened by fundamentalist secularism from the State and undermined by the accommodation with this secularism on the part of its own hierarchy. Sometimes one feels like asking the old question first raised in the Gospels: "Will faith be found on earth?" Yes, faith will be found but, in these times of our complacency, the faith will be guarded by a very few. If there is a comparison with earlier periods to be made, then we are in the Dark Ages when Christians were forced out by prevailing hostility and went underground into the catacombs, or out into the desert.

Increasingly, Christians today are doing similarly. They are forming small groups, saying their prayers, hearing the words of Scripture, studying, preaching and teaching, celebrating the Holy Communion, clinging to one another and to God. In the electronic age, these groups have redefined the idea of a *locality*. Our church of St Michael, here in the City of London has its Sunday congregation, drawn from throughout London and beyond — because we have no resident population in the parish. But we are also a network of Christians in contact through our website which carries news of our programme and much spiritual and theological literature. In this way Christians throughout the country and overseas are put in contact with one another and form something like a congregation in cyberspace, attending church and meeting when they can, but otherwise communicating by e-mail, telephone and letters. Only the technology is new: the sense of a church community, bound together by prayer and friendship, is utterly traditional.

Also, encouragingly, we are finding that old divisions and suspicions among Christians of different denominations and emphases are disappearing in the face of the persecution which threatens us. At St Michael's, Cornhill, we are Prayer Book Anglican-Catholic, but our visiting preachers include Roman Catholics, a Calvinist professor of the philosophy of religion, a Methodist ecumenical officer and several Evangelical ministers. We accommodate the Protestant Proclamation Trust for their annual conference. In all these things we find there is far less to divide us than the solidarity which unites us against a common foe.

So this is what Christians should do: refuse to be discouraged, keep the faith and wait. The desert is not entirely inhospitable. And of course in those early days, it was the desert which produced the Desert Fathers, the beginnings of the monastic movement and the birth of a vigorous new style of Christianity to meet the changed social and political conditions. We should not however be impatient or expect quick results. We are deep into the coming world crisis – a crisis on a scale not seen before. When it comes to timescale and the need for patience, T.S. Eliot said:

"An individual European may not even believe that the Christian Faith is true, but what he says and makes and does will all spring out of this history of European culture and depend upon that culture for its meaning. Only a Christian culture could have produced a Nietzsche or a Voltaire. I do not believe that the culture of Europe could survive the complete disappearance of the Christian Faith. And I am convinced of that not merely because I am a Christian myself, but as a student of social biology. If Christianity goes, the whole of our culture goes. Then you must start painfully again, and you cannot put on a new culture ready-made. You must wait for the grass to grow to feed the sheep to give the wool out of which your new coat will be made. You must pass through many centuries of barbarism."

The Love of God

But what does turning back to God involve? It is not a sorrowful thing. It is not bitter or painful. God is not standing over us with a big stick. It is God's nature to desire the good of his creation. This desire on God's part is eternal and unalterable. No matter how many times we desert him, he will not forsake us. The Bible describes this promise and the relationship which it creates as Covenant. The short way of expressing this is to say that God is love and we are the objects of his love. To return to God is to return home and to be where we belong.

"The love of God comes readily to those who have most need" — says C.H. Sisson. And the love of God is not something distant and ethereal. St Augustine said the best way to understand God's love for us is to think of human love, erotic love, specifically the love between husband and wife. Do we find the comparison even a bit shocking? Well, St Augustine's words often come as a bit of a shock. He said for example: "Love God and do as you like."

For the British the greater part of our difficulties arise out of our character. We are reserved. And the invitation to draw near to God resembles for us the invitation to enter the headmaster's study. We easily imagine God flinging thunderbolts from the top of Mount Sinai. We can imagine *obeying* God — or trying to. But the *love* of God sounds too soppy, too touchy-feely for us. Embarrassing. Perhaps we can just about cope with God's love in the abstract, and see it as a sort of mechanical act of forgiveness, a cancellation of debts; a transaction. But God doesn't want us to keep his commandments because he is bossy or a control freak. God wants us to keep his commandments because they are for our good. The commandments are not abstract legal devices. They are signs of his love.

You will hear preachers say that the Commandments and the Law belong to the Old Testament and that love and grace belong to the New. But the Old Testament is full of examples of love, and these tell us that love is the very heart of God. The late Michael Hyam, former Recorder of London and a Jew, could never read the meeting between Joseph and his brothers without breaking into tears:

150

"Then Joseph could not refrain himself before all them that stood by him; and he cried, Cause every man to go out from me. And there stood no man with him while Joseph made himself known unto his brethren. And he wept aloud. And Joseph said unto his brethren, I am Joseph. Doth my father yet live? And his brethren could not answer him, for they were troubled at his presence."

And again in the Old Testament the prophet Hosea has an unfaithful wife, but he takes her back because he loves her. Hosea says this is how it is between God and his people. At wedding interviews I try to persuade couples to choose a reading from *The Song of Songs* found in the Old Testament. They have to be brave because the love which features there is very sensual:

"Behold thou art fair, my love. Behold thou art fair. Thou hast doves' eyes. Behold thou art fair, my beloved, yea, pleasant. And lo the winter is past, the rain is over and gone. The flowers appear on the earth: the time of the singing of birds is come. My beloved is mine and I am his. By night on my bed I sought him whom my soul loveth."

Be brave then. Be very brave. For this is the love with which God loves you. This ravishing tenderness with which God wants to hold you close to him. When God wants to show us how he loves us, he shows a couple, lovers. And we come into the New Testament where we find that the church is the bride of Christ — "...coming down from God out of heaven, prepared as a bride adorned for her husband."

And then there is that most tender adorable incident in St Luke's Gospel:

"She bringeth an alabaster box of ointment, and stood at his feet behind him weeping and began to wash his feet with her tears and did wipe them with the hairs of her head, and kissed his feet."

This is the love of God. This is how God loves us. Again it is generally believed that the couple Jesus meets on the walk to Emmaus after his resurrection were a married couple and they beseech him: "Abide with us for it is toward evening and the day is far spent."

St Augustine compares God's love to erotic love. This is not the same as lust. Augustine knew all about lust. He knew what it was to be consumed by it:

"Then came I to Carthage, burning, burning. And a cauldron of unholy lusts sang all about my ears."

And he prayed,

"O God make me chaste and continent — but not yet."

But he speaks of his desire for God and his language is erotic, love poetry. And the most passionate you can feel, the all-consuming passion of a teenager in the flush of romantic love — think of Cherubino and that flustered aria in Figaro — *Non so piu* — this passion that will not be denied is only a pale shadow of the passion which God has for you. And again St Augustine says beautifully:

" God loves each of us as though there were only one of us."

And when he speaks of his yearning for God he says,

"I have learnt to love thee late: O Beauty at once so ancient and so new."

This is the relationship with him into which God is calling you. The Passion of Christ is passionate. Isaac Watts was obliged to tone down his great hymn which originally read

"When I survey the wondrous Cross, where the *young* Prince of Glory died."

Creation is God's creation and creation is erotic. That is to say, creation is life. And eros is the love of life in God. God's life. This is why we thrill to see a fine garden — the creation of the first Adam is God's spirit moving in a garden. The Second Adam, Christ, appears first in a garden. Think of *Gerontius* and in the garden secretly ."O wisest love…"

Are you not attracted to God who makes the gardens and the stars and the diatonic scale and gives it to Bach to play with? God who makes the sunrise, the lynxes, the fauns and the snow-capped peaks? All these things that move us so are the handiwork of God. And God's life is emblazoned in them. The sensuality of the world is the created means by which God reaches for us, to touch us. Sensual love, erotic love, is the sacrament which allows us to see through it into the passion of God. The Prayer Book Marriage Service puts it beautifully: With my body I thee worship. The sacrament of marriage is erotic love garlanded by a vow.

We should pray and ask God to make us desire him and want him.

No one puts it better than St Augustine:

"But, what do I love, when I love Thee? Not the prettiness of a body, not the graceful rhythm, not the brightness of light (that friend of these eyes), not the sweet melodies of songs in every style, not the fragrance of flowers and ointments and spices, not manna and honey, not limbs which can be grasped in fleshly embraces - these I do not love, when I love my God. Yet I do love something like a light, a voice, a fragrance, food, embrace of my inner man, wherein for my soul a light shines, and place does not encompass it, where there is a sound which times does not sweep away, where there is a fragrance which the breeze does not disperse, where there is a flavour which eating does not diminish, and where there is a clinging which satiety does not disentwine. This is what I love, when I love my God."

There is nothing to be afraid of, nothing to deter us, nothing to delay us in turning to him. Did not Our Lord say,

"Come unto me all ye that labour and are heavy laden, and I will give you rest. Take my yoke upon you and learn of me; for I am meek and lowly in heart: and ye shall find rest unto your souls.

"For my yoke is easy, and my burden is light" — *St Matthew 11:28-30*